Ajmal Al Qawaa'id

Student's Name: _____

Class / Year: _____

Teacher: _____

School / Madrasah: _____

CONTENTS

Ajmal Al Qawaa'id		Instructions for students	04
		Introduction to Ajmal Al Qawaa'id	06
		Pronunciation Diagram	08
Grade 01:	Lesson 01:	Alphabets	18
Grade 02:	Lesson 02:	Letters in Different Forms	28
Grade 03:	Lesson 03:	Fat-hah	40
	Lesson 04:	Kasrah	42
	Lesson 05:	Dhammah	44
Grade 04:	Lesson 06:	Fat-ha-tayn	50
	Lesson 07:	Kasra-tayn	52
	Lesson 08:	Dhamma-tayn	54
Grade 05:	Lesson 09:	Fat-hah followed by Alif	60
	Lesson 10:	Madd Fat-hah	64
	Lesson 11:	Madd Kasrah	66
	Lesson 12:	Madd Dhammah	68
Grade 06:	Lesson 13:	Sukoon	74
Grade 07:	Lesson 14:	Fat-hah followed by Waw Saakin	80
	Lesson 15:	Dhammah followed by Waw Saakin	82
Grade 08:	Lesson 16:	Fat-hah followed by Ya Saakin	88
	Lesson 17:	Kasrah followed by Ya Saakin	90
Grade 09:	Lesson 18:	Shaddah	98
Grade 10:	Lesson 19:	Silent letters in words	108
	Lesson 20:	Silent Alif	110
	Lesson 21:	Special words	112
	Lesson 22:	Words with a jerking sound	114

Completed on   D D / M M / YEAR

Grade 11:	Lesson 23:	Small Madd	118
	Lesson 24:	Big Madd	120
	Lesson 25:	Big Madd followed by a Shaddah	122
Grade 12:	Lesson 26:	Qalqalah	126
	Lesson 27:	Ghunnah	128
	Lesson 28:	Izhaar	130
Grade 13:	Lesson 29:	Rule of the letter Ra	134
	Lesson 30:	Rule of the word Allaah	136
Grade 14:	Lesson 31:	Idghaam and silent letters	140
	Lesson 32:	Idghaam	142
Grade 15:	Lesson 33:	Ikhfaa	148
	Lesson 34:	Ikhfaa Meem	150
	Lesson 35:	Iqlaab	152
	Lesson 36:	Noon Qutni	154
Grade 16:	Lesson 37:	Stopping on round Ta (Ta Marbootah)	158
	Lesson 38:	Stopping on Fat-ha-tayn	160
	Lesson 39:	Waqf (Stopping)	162
	Lesson 40:	Waqf (Stopping) on three words	164
	Lesson 41:	Saktah	166
Grade 17:	Lesson 42:	Advance stopping and Sajdah	170
	Lesson 43:	Huroof Al-Muqatta'aat	172
	Lesson 44:	Complete Verse Fluency	174
Grade 18:	Lesson 45:	Last 10 Surahs	180

Comments

INSTRUCTIONS FOR STUDENTS

 Do Wudhu before reading your Qaa'idah.

 Come early and refresh your lesson before reading to your teacher.

 Sit with respect infront of your teacher.

 Whenever beginning the session read Ta'awwudh (A'oodhu Billaahe Minash Shaytaanir Rajeem). Always start reading your lesson with Tasmiyah (Bismillaahir Rahmaanir Raheem).

 Point at the word you're reading with your right index finger.

 Avoid only reading your lesson once or twice. Keep practicing until you're called to read to the teacher so you progress to the next lesson.

   Completed on D D / M M / YEAR

 Always listen to the teacher attentively whilst they are explaining the lesson.

 If you do not understand the lesson ask the teacher to explain it until you understand.

 Always put your hand up if you want to ask the teacher anything.

 Never disrespect the teacher by speaking back to them.

 Avoid speaking unnecessarily to your friends during your learning time.

 Ensure that you are wearing the correct uniform and that you have all your learning resources with you.

 Remind yourself of all the beautiful rewards of learning the Qur'aan.

INTRODUCTION TO AJMAL AL QAWAA'ID

This book has been designed to help make reading the Qur'aan easy. It is important to understand why certain tools have been included and how to make use of them.

The Grades
This book has been divided into 18 grades. Gradually preparing the student by building solid foundations before progressing to the advance rules.
Each grade is a foundation for the following grade. It is important that each level is mastered before progressing to the next.

The Overview
This is a teacher/parent section where each lesson will be explained in detail. Teachers will know what needs to be taught and how. Parents will know exactly what their child's targets are and how to support their learning at home.

The Arabic page
This is the most important page in the book and needs to be learnt properly. Each page has its own learning objective and targets hence requires lots of practice.

The Star reward system and completed on section

At the bottom of the Arabic page there will be 'three stars' that will be used by teachers to monitor progress regularly. Once the lesson is completed the date will be written on the 'completed on' section by the teacher.

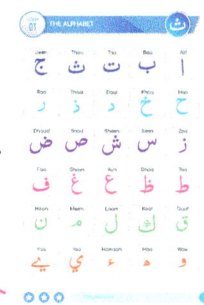

 = Requires more practice

 = Completed with assistance but needs some practice

= Independently completed and ready to move on

Step by step

This section will explain the Arabic page step by step in detail. Looking at the Arabic page and reading the relevant part of this section together will make the learning and understanding easier.

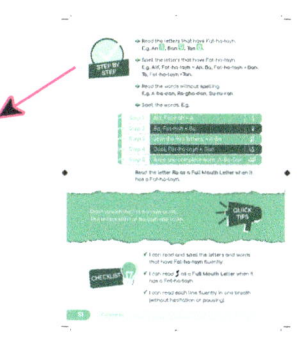

Quick tips

This section will include valuable guidance from experienced teachers.

Checklist

This self-assessment section needs to be completed by the student before progressing onto the next lesson.

Comments

Parents and teachers can comment as and when required.

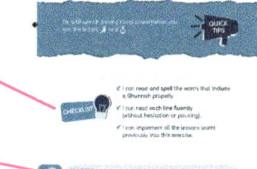

PRONUNCIATION DIAGRAM

Every letter is pronounced from a specific part of the mouth and throat. Take a look at each letters origin point and familiarise yourself with them.

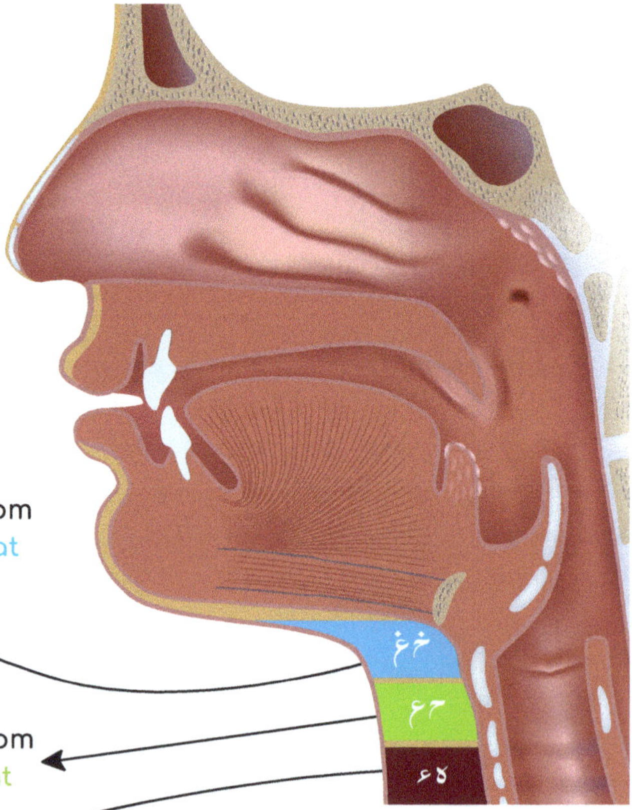

خ غ Sound produced from the Top of the Throat

ع ح Sound produced from the Middle of Throat

ء ه Sound produced from the Bottom of the Throat

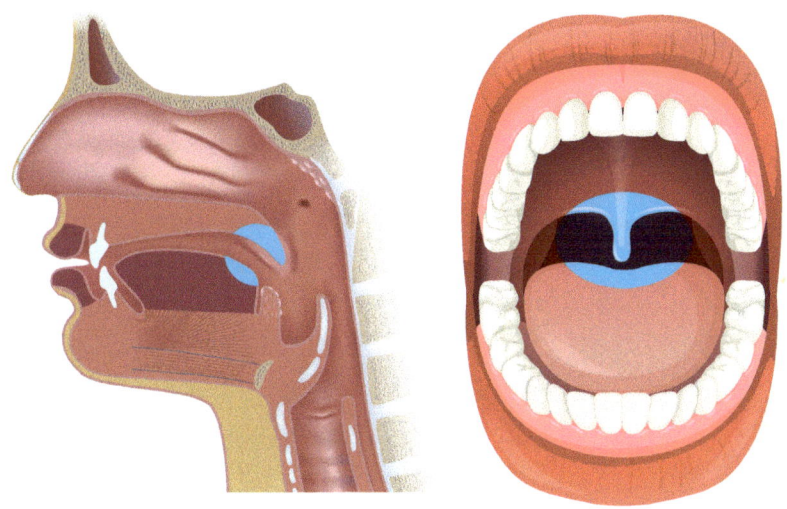

ق – **Back of the Tongue** to touch the roof of the Mouth.

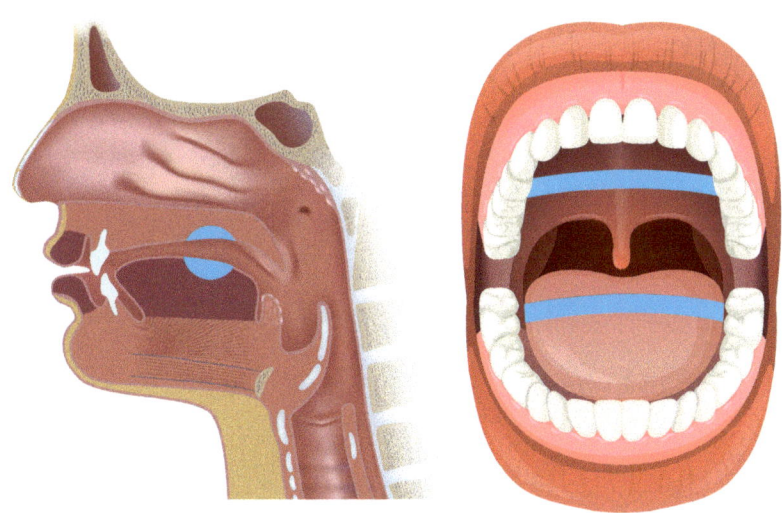

ك – **Middle of the tongue but closer to the back** to touch the roof of the mouth.

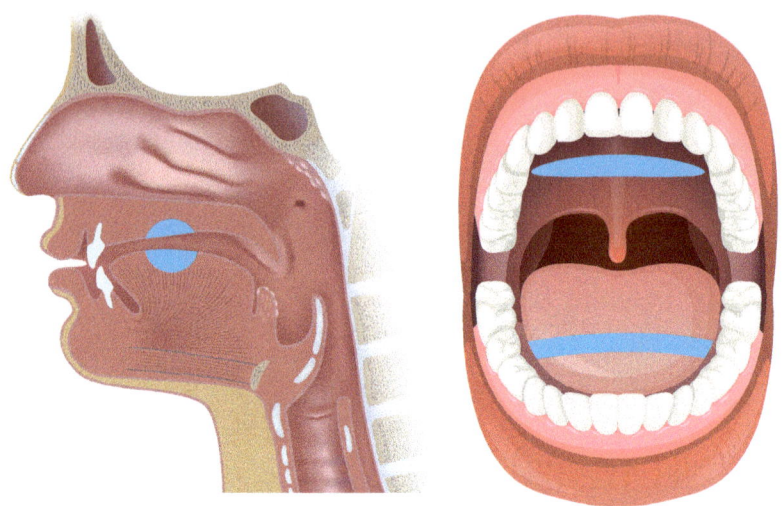

ج ش ى – **Middle of the tongue but closer to the front** to touch the roof of the mouth.

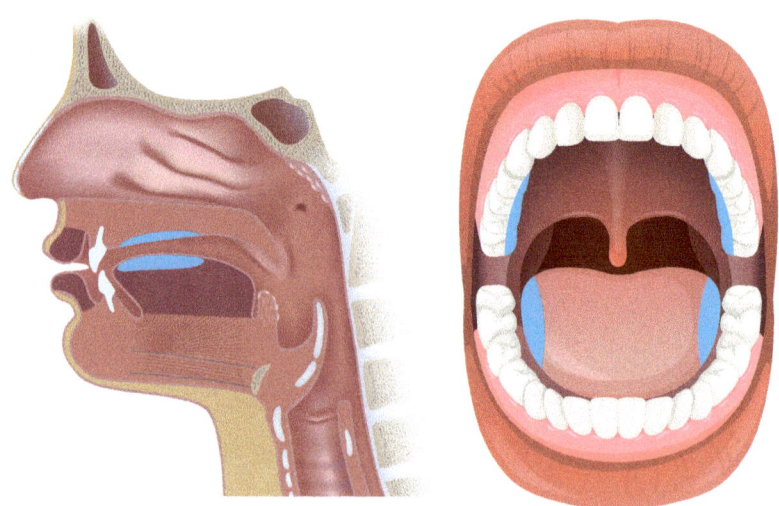

ض – **Side of the tongue** to touch the top back teeth.

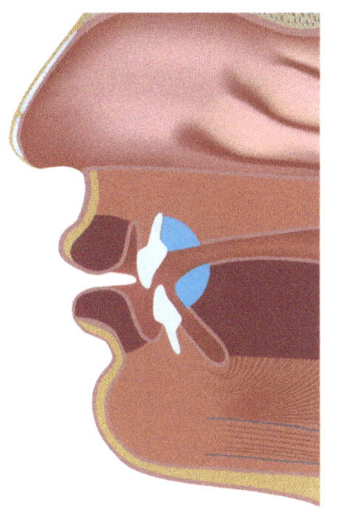
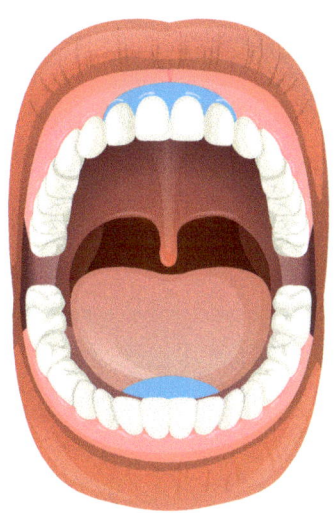

ل – **Tip of the tongue (flat)** to touch the gums of the top front teeth.

ن – **Tip of the tongue (flat)** to touch the gums of the top front teeth.

ر – **Tip and edge of the tongue** to touch the gums of the top teeth.

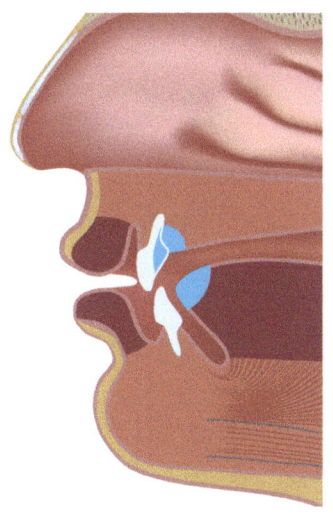
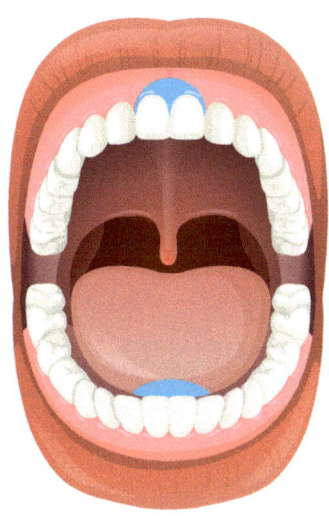

ط د ت – **Tip of the tongue** to touch the root of the top front 2 teeth.

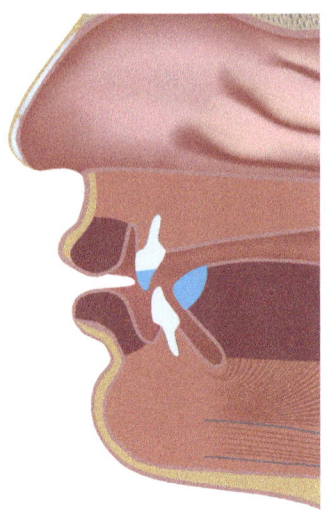
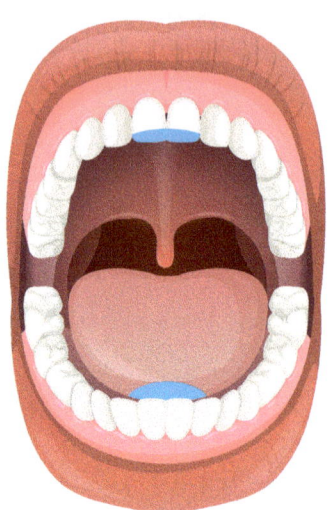

ث ذ ظ - **Tip of the tongue** to touch the tip of the top front 2 teeth.

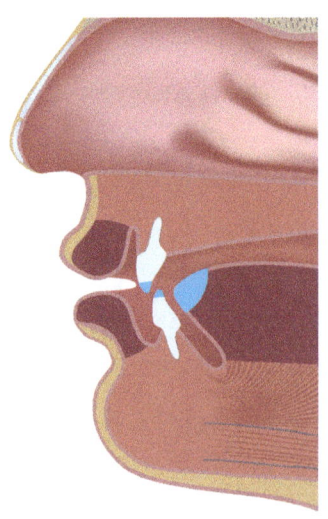
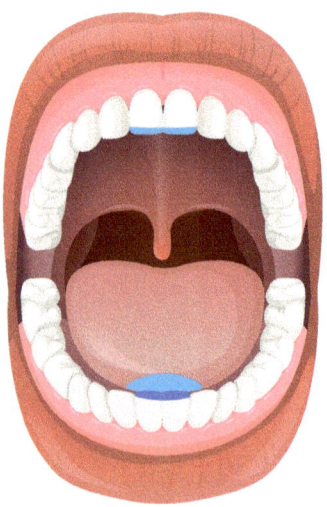

س ز ص - **Tip of the tongue** to touch the edge of the bottom 2 teeth whilst slightly touching the top 2 teeth as well.

Completed on

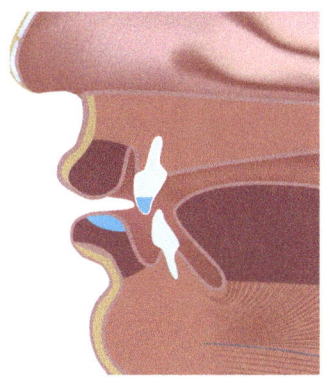 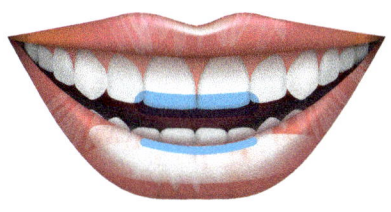

ف – **The inner part of the lower lip** to touch the tip of the top two teeth.

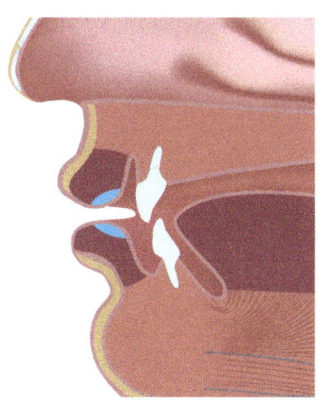 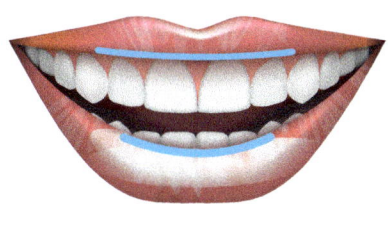

ب – **The inner part of both lips** to touch each other.

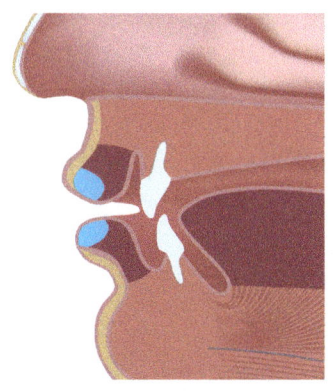 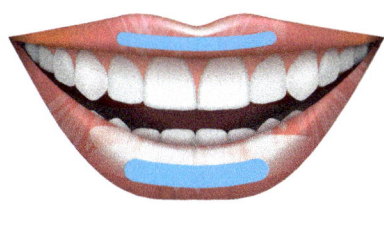

م – **The Outer part of both lips** to touch each other.

Notes

GRADE 01

The Prophet ﷺ said:

"The best amongst you is he who learns the Qur'aan and teaches it to others."

(Bukhaari)

OVERVIEW

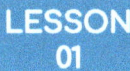 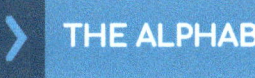 

LESSON 01 > THE ALPHABET

- Each letter should be **pronounced correctly**.
- Students must be able to identify and recognise each letter correctly i.e. with its dots, similarities and differences in shapes etc.
- Students must memorise the entire alphabet with its **correct pronunciation**.
- Students must memorise the entire alphabet by reading the letters and **mentioning how many dots each letter has** i.e. Alif has no dots, Baa has one dot below, Taa has two dots above etc.
- To build fluency the teacher may point out a random letter and ask the student to identify it.

EXERCISE 01 Full Mouth Letters

- The student must be able to **identify** and **read** the **full mouth letters** correctly with confidence. The full mouth letters are highlighted in blue.

EXERCISE 02 Mixed Alphabets

- The student must be able to read the **mixed alphabets** with **confidence** and with **fluency**.

LESSON 01: THE ALPHABET

Alif	Baa	Taa	Thaa	Jeem
ا	ب	ت	ث	ج

Haa	Khaa	Daal	Thaal	Raa
ح	خ	د	ذ	ر

Zaa	Seen	Sheen	Saad	Dhaad
ز	س	ش	ص	ض

Taa	Dhaa	'Ayn	Ghayn	Faa
ط	ظ	ع	غ	ف

Qaaf	Kaaf	Laam	Meem	Noon
ق	ك	ل	م	ن

Waw	Haa	Hamzah	Yaa	Yaa
و	ه	ء	ي	ىے

Completed on DD / MM / YEAR

- Identify **each letter** with its correct pronunciation.
- Read the **entire alphabet** fluently from memory.
- Recognise the differences in the shapes of the letters.

- Recognise, learn and memorise the alphabet by reading each letter.
  E.g. **Alif,** has no dots
  Baa, has one dot at the bottom
  Taa, has two dots on top
  This will aid your letter recognition.

- The best way to memorise the letters is to have interesting links to them.
  E.g. The smiley face letter = ت
  The amazing letter = و
  The snake letter = س
  (make your own)

- I can read the entire **Arabic alphabet fluently.**
- I can **pronounce** all the letters correctly.
- I can **recognise** the differences in the **shapes of the letters** and the number of dots they have from memory fluently.

EXERCISE 01 — FULL MOUTH LETTERS خ

ج	ث	ت	ب	ا
ر	ذ	د	**خ**	ح
ض	**ص**	ش	س	ز
ف	**غ**	ع	**ظ**	**ط**
ن	م	ل	ك	**ق**
ے	ي	ء	ه	و

Completed on DD / MM / YEAR

- ▶ **Identify** each **full mouth letter** with its correct pronunciation.
- ▶ Read the entire **full mouth letters** fluently from memory.
- ▶ Recognise the **differences in the shapes** of the letters.

Read the **full mouth letters** as if your mouth is full of food or full of air.

- ✓ I can recognise and pronounce all the **full mouth letters** properly.
- ✓ I can read the entire alphabet aloud **from memory**.
- ✓ I can implement all the lessons learnt previously into this exercise.

EXERCISE 02 — MIXED ALPHABETS

ح	ت	ا	ب	ج	ط	ذ	ز
خ	ظ	غ	ع	ق	ض	ث	ش
ف	و	م	ے	ک	ء	د
ن	ر	ص	ل	س	ق	ذ	ب
ا	ف	ک	د	غ	ث	ح	ظ
ض	م	ج	و	ي	ء	ع	ش
ن	ج	ذ	ع	ص	ے	ل	ط
ت	ر	غ	ث	ح	ف	ق	ظ
ک	و	م	ش	ء	ع	ي	ض

STEP BY STEP

- Read out all the letters **fluently** with their correct pronunciation.

- Read one **entire line** without hesitation or pausing.

- Recognise the **differences in the shapes** of the letters.

QUICK TIPS

- Read in random order, pointing at random letters and read them as quickly as possible.

- Keep reading the letters in groups of 3 until your speed increases, then do the next group until you have read the whole line.

CHECKLIST

- I can read all the letters in **mixed form** without referring back to the previous pages.

- I can read an **entire line without pausing**.

- I can implement all previous lessons learnt into this exercise.

Comments

Notes

GRADE 02

The Prophet ﷺ said:

"Verily, Allaah elevates some people with this Qur'aan and lowers others."

(Muslim)

OVERVIEW

LESSON 02 > LETTERS IN DIFFERENT FORMS

- This lesson shows how each letter is written in different forms i.e. at the **beginning, middle and end of each word**.
- Ask the student to identify the similarities between the **joint form letters** and the large letters (dots, shapes etc).
- The letters **Raa** ر and **Zaa** ز are also written like this: **Raa** ٧ **Zaa** ٧

EXERCISE 01 — Special letters ا د ذ ر ز و and Single form letters

- The **Special Letters** do not join with **letters that come after them**, examples of these letters not joining are given in the words (Page 30).
- The student should build fluency in identifying **single letters** before moving on to the **two letter words**, then **three letter words** etc.
- Advanced students may attempt to identify all the letters.

EXERCISE 02 — Dual and Plural letters

- Further explain how the letters are joined to make words.
- The gaps between the letters in the first two lines are there to help distinguish each letter.
- The student should not hesitate or pause when reading the words.
- The student may refer to previous lessons as guidance particularly with identifying the **Special Letters**.

EXERCISE 03 — Extension

- The students should be able to identify and pronounce each letter correctly.
- Each line must be read without any hesitation or pausing. The student should be encouraged to attempt reading the word quickly and accurately.
- This will help build fluency and consistency in their recitation.
- Students must be **confident** in recognising all the **different forms of letters** by this stage before progressing on to the next grade.

LESSON 02: LETTERS IN DIFFERENT FORMS

ا	ب	ت	ث	ج
ا ا ا	ب ب ب	ت ت ت ة	ث ث ث	ج ج ج

ح	خ	د	ذ	ر
ح ح ح	خ خ خ	د ـد ـد	ذ ـذ ـذ	ر ـر ـر

ز	س	ش	ص	ض
ز ـز ـز	س ـس ـس	ش ـش ـش	ص ـص ـص	ض ـض ـض

ط	ظ	ع	غ	ف
ط ـط ـط	ظ ـظ ـظ	ع ـع ـع	غ ـغ ـغ	ف ـف ـف

ق	ك	ل	م	ن
ق ـق ـق	ك ـك ـك	ل ـل ـل	م ـم ـم	ن ـن ـن

و	ه	ء	ي	ـے
و ـو ـو	ه ـه ـه	ء ـئ ـئ	ي ـي ـي	ـے ـے ـے

Completed on D·D / M·M / YEAR

- ▸ Recognise the **letters in different forms**.
- ▸ Read each line **without pausing**.
- ▸ Identify the similarities between the Single Form Letters and the Joint Form Letters.

- ▸ Identify the similarities between the Single Form Letters and the Joint Form Letters using the dots method.
- ▸ Remember! When the letter **Yaa** ى is written at the end of a word, it may not have any dots.
- ▸ Also the letter **Raa** and **Zaa** are sometimes written ٫ and ٫̇ .

- ⊙ I can identifiy all the **letters in different forms**.
- ⊙ I can read the letters in **different forms** without hesitation or pausing.
- ⊙ I can implement all the lessons learnt previously into this exercise.

EXERCISE 01 — SPECIAL LETTERS

ا	د	ذ	ر	ز	و
↓	↓	↓	↓	↓	↓
احد	دكا	ذهب	رفع	زعم	وجد

| احد | دكا | ذهب | رفع | زعم | وجد |

SINGLE FORM LETTERS

ش	ظ	غ	م	خ	ك	ج	ت
ل	ض	ب	ﺋ	و	س	ف	ذ
ح	ع	ز	ث	ر	ن	ي	ص
ق	ه	د	ط	ك	ه	ف	ﺋ
ل	ض	ن	ق	ب	ع	ظ	ت

Completed on D D / M M / YEAR

- ▸ Recognise the **Special Letters** and understand their roles

- ▸ Read the **Single Form Letters** in standalone form

- ▸ Read **two letter words** fluently and accurately

Remember, **Alif** for Allaah, **Daal, Thaal, Ra, Za** come together and finally **Waw**. Wow! for learning the 'Special Letters'.

- ✓ I can recognise all the **Special Letters**.
- ✓ I can read all the **Joint Form Letters** clearly and fluently.
- ✓ I can implement all the lessons learnt previously into this exercise.

EXERCISE 02 — TWO LETTER WORDS

طه	يس	حم	فة	غق	ثذ
طس	خع	لد	مغ	نض	طل
بي	تي	ثي	لي	ني	يي
بي	تي	ثي	لي	ني	يي

THREE LETTER WORDS

يحب	تمت	سنن	لكن	حزب	نهى
تحت	نخل	عجل	يحى	لوح	تجد
فتح	لبث	عوج	لحق	جبل	خزى
بخل	مهد	داع	جمع	هاد	حجج

STEP BY STEP

- ▸ Read the letters fluently when written together to form words. E.g. 'Taa', 'Haa'.
- ▸ Read **two letter words** fluently and accurately.
- ▸ Recognise the letters 'Baa', 'Taa', 'Thaa', 'Laam', 'Noon' and 'Yaa', when written together with a 'Yaa'.

- ▸ Put a line through the join and remember that the top letter comes first and it's dots would be on it or below it. The top letter would either be a Baa, Taa, Thaa, Laam, Noon or Yaa depending on where the dots are.
- ▸ The letter below will be a Yaa. Yaa is written without its dots when it comes at the end of the word.
- ▸ Practice one line at a time as **quickly as possible**, keep repeating it until your speed increases. Then move onto the next one.

QUICK TIPS

CHECKLIST

- ✓ I can recognise **all the letters** when written as a word.
- ✓ I can read the letters when written as a word **fluently in one breath.**
- ✓ I can implement all previous lessons learnt into this exercise.

EXERCISE 03 — EXTENSION

بـ	تـ	ثـ	نـ	يـ
خـ	حـ	جـ		

| يَجْعَل | نَجْنِى | نَخْلَة | وَنَخْل | نَجِيَّا |
| يجعل | نجنى | نخلة | ونخل | نجيا |

| بِخْبِر | تَخْزَنَّا | بَخْلُوا | جَبَل | يُخَفَّف |
| بخبر | تخزنا | بخلوا | جبل | يخفف |

| نَخِيل | تَخْفَى | يَخْلِف | تَجْرِى | يُجِير |
| نخيل | تخفى | يخلف | تجرى | يجير |

| يَجْتَبِى | انْجَيْنَا | يَخْتَص | ثُجَاجًا | يُحْيِين |
| يجتبى | انجينا | يختص | ثجاجا | يحيين |

STEP BY STEP

- Read out all the letters fluently with their correct pronunciation.
- Read one entire line **without taking a breath** (without hesitation or pausing).
- Recognise the letters 'Ba', 'Jeem', 'Kha', 'Noon', when written together.

بخبر تخزنا ثجاجا نجنى يخفف

QUICK TIPS

- Put a line through the join and remember that the top letter comes first and it's dots would be on it or below it.
- The top letter would either be a Baa, Taa, Thaa, Noon or Yaa depending on the dots.
- The letter below will either be a Jeem, Ha or Kha.

CHECKLIST

- I can read all the letters in **mixed form** without referring back to the previous pages.
- I can **read an entire line** without pausing.
- I can implement all previous lessons learnt into this exercise.

Comments

Notes

The Prophet ﷺ said:

"Read the Qur'aan, for it will come as an intercessor for its reciters on the Day of Resurrection."

(Muslim)

OVERVIEW

LESSON 03 — FAT-HAH

The Fat-hah gives an **A** sound and **should not be stretched**.
- The letter Ra will be pronounced as a **Full Mouth Letter** when it has a Fat-hah above it: رَ
- The letters Ra ر and Za ز are also written like this: ڔ ڒ
- The letter Ya ى does not always come with dots, so familiarise yourself with the shape.

Harakaat = Symbols (such as Fat-hah, Kasrah, Dhammah etc).

LESSON 04 — KASRAH

The Kasrah gives an **E** sound and **should not be stretched**.
- The letter Ra will be pronounced as an Empty Mouth Letter when it has a Kasrah beneath it: رِ
- The letters Ra ر and Za ز are also written like this: ڔ ڒ
- The letter Ya ى does not always come with dots, so familiarise yourself with the shape.

LESSON 05 — DHAMMAH

The Dhammah gives an **U** sound and **should not be stretched**.
- The letter **Ra** will be pronounced as an Full Mouth Letter when it has a Dhammah above it: رُ
- The letters Ra ر and Za ز are also written like this: ڔ ڒ
- The letter Ya ى does not always come with dots, so familiarise yourself with the shape.

* Extension = More practice before progressing further.

LESSON 03 — FAT-HAH

اَ	بَ	تَ	ثَ	جَ	حَ	خَ	دَ
ذَ	رَ	زَ	سَ	شَ	صَ	ضَ	طَ
ظَ	عَ	غَ	فَ	قَ	كَ	لَ	مَ
نَ	وَ	هَ	ءَ	یَ			

EXERCISE

فَصَلَ	هَلَكَ	حَذَرَ	كَتَبَ	سَبَقَ
ذَرَأَ	عَبَسَ	طَبَعَ	وَهَنَ	بَسَمَ
وَزَرَ	شَرَحَ	سَقَرَ	فَعَلَ	وَقَعَ
حَجَرَ	وَهَبَ	خَلَقَ	رَفَثَ	شَجَرَ
مَعَكَ	كَشَفَ	دَخَلَ	وَظَهَرَ	فَخَرَجَ

STEP BY STEP

- Read the letters that have Fat-hah.
  E.g. "A" أَ, "Ba" بَ, "Ta" تَ.

- Spell the letters that have a Fat-hah.
  E.g. Alif, Fat-hah = A. Ba, Fat-hah = Ba.
  Ta, Fat-hah = Ta.

- Read the words.
  E.g. Fa-Sa-La, Ha-La-Ka, Ha-Tha-Ra.

- Spell the words that have Fat-hah. E.g.

Step 1	Fa, Fat-hah = Fa	فَ
Step 2	Saad, Fat-hah = Sa	صَ
Step 3	Join the two, Fa-Sa	فَصَ
Step 4	Laam, Fat-hah = La	لَ
Step 5	Read the entire word, Fa-Sa-La	فَصَلَ

Read the letter **Ra as a Full Mouth Letter** when it has a Fat-hah.

QUICK TIPS

- **Don't stretch** the Fat-hah at all.

- The letters with Fat-hah all end with the sound A.

CHECKLIST

- I can read and spell the **letters and words** that have a **Fat-hah** fluently.

- I can read the letter **Ra as a Full Mouth Letter** when it has a Fat-hah.

- I can read each line fluently in one breath (without hesitation or pausing).

 **LESSON 04 — KASRAH**

اِ	بِ	تِ	ثِ	جِ	حِ	خِ	دِ	ذِ	رِ

زِ	سِ	شِ	صِ	ضِ	طِ	ظِ	عِ	غِ	فِ

قِ	كِ	لِ	مِ	نِ	وِ	هِ	ءِ	يِ

EXERCISE

كِبَرِ	حَفِظَ	تَرِنَ	شِيَةَ	آمِنَ
اِبِلَ	عَلِمَ	اِرَمَ	فَلِمَ	آبَتِ
بَلَدِ	مَلِكِ	وَسِعَ	حَطِبَ	كَرِهَ
وَعَمِلَ	وَوَرِثَ	وَقَعَتِ	يَئِسَ	شِيَعِ
لِخَزَنَتِ	بِيَدِكَ	أَفَأَمِنَ	بِعِصَمِ	وَخَسِئَ

STEP BY STEP

- Read the letters that have Kasrah.
  E.g. E اِ , Be بِ , Te تِ .

- Spell the letters that have Kasrah.
  E.g. Alif, Kasrah = E. Ba, Kasrah = Be.
  Ta, Kasrah = Te.

- Read the words.
  E.g. A-Me-Na, She-Ya-Ta, Ta-Ra-Ne.

- Spell the words that have Kasrah. E.g.

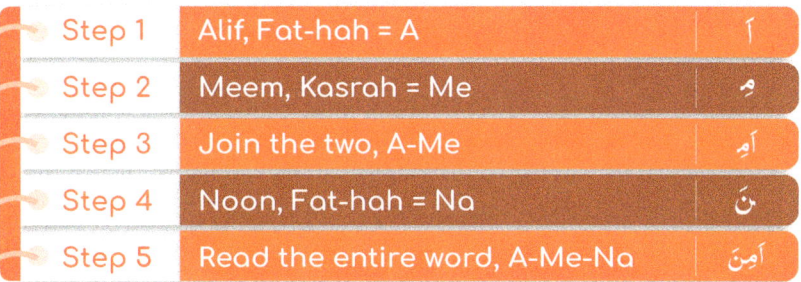

Step 1	Alif, Fat-hah = A	اَ
Step 2	Meem, Kasrah = Me	مِ
Step 3	Join the two, A-Me	اَمِ
Step 4	Noon, Fat-hah = Na	نَ
Step 5	Read the entire word, A-Me-Na	اَمِنَ

Read the letter **Ra** as an **Empty Mouth Letter** when it has a Kasrah.

QUICK TIPS

- **Don't stretch** the Fat-hah and Kasrah at all.
- The letters with Kasrah all end with the sound **E**.

CHECKLIST

- I can read and spell the **letters and words** that have a **Kasrah** fluently.
- I can read each line **fluently in one breath** (without any hesitation or pausing).
- I can Implement all the lessons learnt previously into this exercise.

LESSON 05 — DHAMMAH

اُ	بُ	تُ	ثُ	جُ	حُ	خُ	دُ	ذُ	رُ

زُ	سُ	شُ	صُ	ضُ	طُ	ظُ	عُ	غُ	فُ

قُ	كُ	لُ	مُ	نُ	وُ	هُ	ءُ	ىُ

EXERCISE

لُعِنَ	يَعِدُ	هُدِىَ	اَجِدُ	نُفِخَ
حُبِّك	اَعِظُ	حُشِىَ	تَجِدُ	يَرِثُ
سُبُلَ	ذُكِرَ	سُقِطَ	أُخَرُ	قُضِىَ
وُضِعَ	كَبُرَ	نُقِرَ	بُغِىَ	عُفِىَ
يَعِدُ	أُذُن	كُبِتَ	خَبُثَ	أُفِكَ

STEP BY STEP

- Read the letters that have a Dhammah.
  E.g. U ُا , Bu بُ , Tu تُ .

- Spell the letters that have Dhammah.
  E.g. Alif, Dhammah = U. Ba, Dhammah = Bu.
  Ta, Dhammah = Tu.

- Read the words.
  E.g. Lu-'E-Na, Ya-'E-Du, Hu-De-Ya.

- Spell the words that have Dhammah. E.g.

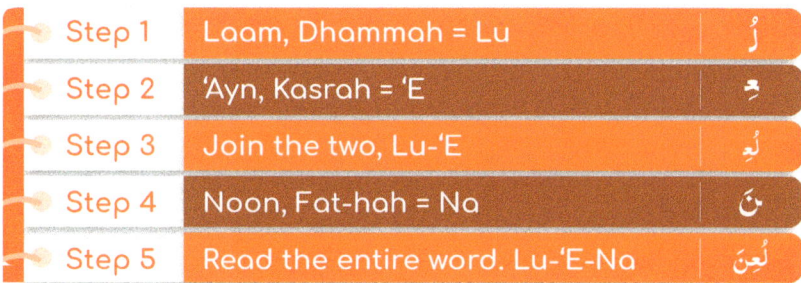

Step 1	Laam, Dhammah = Lu	لُ
Step 2	'Ayn, Kasrah = 'E	عِ
Step 3	Join the two, Lu-'E	لُعِ
Step 4	Noon, Fat-hah = Na	نَ
Step 5	Read the entire word. Lu-'E-Na	لُعِنَ

Read the letter **Ra** as a **Full Mouth Letter** when it has a **Dhammah**.

QUICK TIPS

- **Don't stretch** the **Fat-hah, Kasrah** and **Dhammah** at all.
- As soon as you point at a word you should be able to read it without thinking for too long. The letters with Dhammah all end with the sound **U**.

CHECKLIST

- I can read and spell the **letters and words** that have a **Dhammah** fluently.

- I can read the letter **Ra** as a **Full Mouth Letter** when it has a **Dhammah**.

- I can read each line **fluently in one breath** (without any hesitation or pausing).

Comments

LESSON 03-05 — EXTENSION

رَفَعَ	وُجِدَ	ذَكَرَ	قَمَرَ	يَكُ	
نَظَرَ	مَثَلُ	كُتِبَ	ظَلَمَ	عَدَلَ	
تَزِرُ	كَسَبَ	صَدَقَ	سَبَقَ	زَعَمَ	

تَرَكَ	يَرِثُ	عَهِدَ	وَجَدَ	قُتِلَ	
زُبُرِ	جَرَمَ	كُفِرَ	رَدِفَ	شَهِدَ	
ذَهَبَ	وَنُذُرِ	بَعَثَ	ضَرَبَ	قُدِرَ	

عَمَلُكَ	كَلِمَتُ	فَنَذَرُ	لَنُبِذَ	صُحُفِ	
فَبَصَرُكَ	عَضُدَكَ	خَلَقَكَ	وَتَصِفُ	فَجُمِعَ	

STEP BY STEP

- ▸ Read and spell all the words **fluent**ly with their correct pronunciation.
- ▸ Read an entire line without taking a breath.

QUICK TIPS

- ▸ Read in a random order, pointing at random letters and reading them as quickly as possible.
- ▸ Harakaat = Symbols (such as Fat-hah, Kasrah, Dhammah etc).

CHECKLIST

- ✓ I can read all the words that have **Fat-hah, Kasrah and Dhammah** fluently.
- ✓ I can read an entire line without pausing.
- ✓ I can implement all previous lessons learnt into this exercise.

Comments

GRADE 04

The Prophet ﷺ said:
"Whoever reads the Qur'aan and memorises it, Allaah will admit him to Paradise and allow him to intercede for ten of his family members who all deserved to enter Hell."

(Ibn Majah)

OVERVIEW

Fat-ha-tayn is a Fat-hah sound with an **N sound** at the end and should not be stretched.
(Fat-ha-tayn always comes at the end of a word, and mostly with an Alif).
- ▶ The letter Ra will be pronounced as a Full Mouth Letter when it has a Fat-ha-tayn above it: رً
- ▶ The letters Ra ر and Za ز are also written like this: ں ں
- ▶ The letter Ya ى does not always come with dots, so familiarise yourself with the shape.

Kasra-tayn is a Kasrah sound with an **N sound** at the end and should not be stretched. (Kasra-tayn always comes at the end of a word).
- ▶ The letter Ra will be pronounced as a Empty Mouth Letter when it has a Kasra-tayn beneath it: رٍ
- ▶ The letters Ra ر and Za ز are also written like this: ں ں
- ▶ The letter Ya ى does not always come with dots, so familiarise yourself with the shape.

Dhamma-tayn is a Dhammah sound with an **N sound** at the end and should not be stretched. (Dhamma-tayn always comes at the end of a word).
- ▶ The letter Ra will be pronounced as a Full Mouth Letter when it has a Dhamma-tayn above it: رٌ
- ▶ The letters Ra ر and Za ز are also written like this: ں ں
- ▶ The letter Ya ى does not always come with dots, so familiarise yourself with the shape.

Note: Tanween = Fat-ha-tayn, Kasra-tayn and Dhamma-tayn.

*Extension = More practice before progressing further.

LESSON 06 — FAT-HA-TAYN

أَ بًا تًا ثًا جًا حًا خًا دًا ذًا رًا

زًا سًا شًا صًا ضًا طًا ظًا عًا غًا فًا

قًا كًا لًا مًا نًا وًا هًا ئًا يًا

EXERCISE

آبَدًا رَغَدًا سُرًا حَزَنًا ذُلُلًا

عَضُدًا سَكَرًا عِوَجًا مَلِكًا سَعَةً

طَرَفًا صَعِقًا شُهُبًا سَكَنًا قَدَرًا

شَطَطًا خَطَئًا لُبَدًا نُزُلًا وَزُلَفًا

آمَنَةً حَسَنَةً بَقَرَةً وَحَفَدَةً صَدَقَةً

    Completed on   /   /

STEP BY STEP

- Read the letters that have Fat-ha-tayn.
  E.g. An ﺃ, Ban ﺑًـ, Tan ﺗًـ.

- Spell the letters that have Fat-ha-tayn.
  E.g. Alif, Fat-ha-tayn = An. Ba, Fat-ha-tayn = Ban.
  Ta, Fat-ha-tayn =Tan.

- Read the words without spelling.
  E.g. A-ba-dan, Ra-gha-dan, Su-ru-ran.

- Spell the words. E.g.

Step 1	Alif, Fat-hah = A	اَ
Step 2	Ba, Fat-hah = Ba	بَ
Step 3	Join the two letters, = A-Ba	اَبَ
Step 4	Daal, Fat-ha-tayn = Dan	دًا
Step 5	Read the complete word, A-Ba-Dan	اَبَدًا

Read the letter **Ra** as a **Full Mouth Letter** when it has a Fat-ha-tayn.

QUICK TIPS

- Don't stretch the Fat-ha-tayn at all.

- The letters with Fat-ha-tayn end in An.

CHECKLIST

- ✓ I can read and spell the letters and words that have **Fat-ha-tayn** fluently.

- ✓ I can read ﺭ as a **Full Mouth Letter** when it has a Fat-ha-tayn.

- ✓ I can read each line fluently in one breath (without hesitation or pausing).

LESSON 07 — KASRA-TAYN

اِ بِ تِ ثِ جِ حِ خِ دِ ذِ رِ

زِ سِ شِ صِ ضِ طِ ظِ عِ غِ فِ

قِ كِ لِ مِ نِ وِ هِ ءِ يِ

EXERCISE

أُمَمٍ فِئَةٍ خَبَرٍ حَمًا لِسَبَا

بَرَدٍ سَنَةٍ سَحًى شَجَرٍ سُرَارٍ

فُرُشٍ سُوَرٍ مَطًا وَسُعُرٍ وَدُسُرٍ

بِسَحًى سَفَرَةٍ هُمَزَةٍ رَقَبَةٍ ثَمَرَةٍ

بِصَدَقَةٍ بِسَخَطٍ بِغَضَبٍ لُمَزَةٍ بَرَرَةٍ

STEP BY STEP

- Read the letters that have Kasra-tayn.
  E.g. In ٍ, Bin ٍ, Tin ٍ.

- Spell the letters that have Kasra-tayn.
  E.g. Alif, Kasra-tayn = In. Ba, Kasra-tayn = Bin.
  Ta, Kasra-tayn = Tin.

- Read the words without spelling.
  E.g. U-ma-min, Fe-a-tin, Kha-ba-rin.

- Spell the words. E.g.

Step 1	Alif, Dhammah = U	أُ
Step 2	Meem, Fat-hah = Ma	مَ
Step 3	Join the two letters, U-Ma	أُمَ
Step 4	Meem Kasra-tayn = Min	مٍ
Step 5	Read the complete word = U-Ma-Min	أُمَمٍ

QUICK TIPS

- Don't stretch the Fat-ha-tayn and Kasra-tayn at all.

- The letters with Kasra-tayn end in 'In'.

CHECKLIST

- ✓ I can read and spell the letters and words which have **Kasra-tayn** fluently.

- ✓ I can read each line **fluently in one breath** (without hesitation or pausing).

- ✓ I can implement all the lessons learnt previously into this exercise.

LESSON 08: DHAMMA-TAYN

اٌ بٌ تٌ ثٌ جٌ حٌ خٌ دٌ ذٌ رٌ
زٌ سٌ شٌ صٌ ضٌ طٌ ظٌ عٌ غٌ فٌ
قٌ كٌ لٌ مٌ نٌ وٌ هٌ ءٌ ىٌ

EXERCISE

اَشٍ	حُمْرٌ	مَلَاٌ	قَتَرٌ	اَخٌ
سُنَنٌ	فِئَةٌ	وَلَدٌ	قِطَعٌ	سَكَنٌ
نَجَسٌ	لَفِرَحٌ	نَصْبٌ	كُتُبٌ	غُرَفٌ
جُدَدٌ	حُرُمٌ	سِنَةٌ	خُشُبٌ	وَبِيَعٌ
فَعَجَبٌ	فَرَجُلٌ	وَجِلَةٌ	فَنَظْرَةٌ	كَلِمَةٌ

STEP BY STEP

- Read the letters that have Dhamma-tayn.
  E.g. Oon, Boon, Toon.

- Spell the letters that have Dhamma-tayn.
  E.g. Alif, Dhamma-tayn = Oon. Ba, Dhamma-tayn = Boon. Ta, Dhamma-tayn = Toon.

- Read the words without spelling.
  E.g. A-khoon, Qa-ta-roon, Ma-la-oon.

- Spell the words. E.g.

Step 1	Alif, Fat-hah = A	ﺃ
Step 2	Kha, Dhamma-tayn = Khoon	خٌ
Step 3	Read the complete word, A-Khoon	أخٌ

Read the letter **Ra** as a **Full Mouth Letter** when it has a Dhamma-tayn.

QUICK TIPS

- Don't stretch the Fat-ha-tayn, Kasra-tayn and Dhamma-tayn at all.

- The letters with Dhamma-tayn end in Oon.

CHECKLIST

- I can read and spell the letters and words that have **Dhamma-tayn** fluently.

- I can read ر as a **Full Mouth Letter** when it has a Dhamma-tayn.

- I can read each line fluently in one breath (without hesitation or pausing).

EXERCISE 06-08: EXTENSION

مَثَلًا	بَشَّ	ذَهَبًا	نَكِدًا	اَحَدٍ
بِدَمٍ	كُفُوًا	اَسِفًا	لَبَنًا	حَرَجٍ
مَلِكٌ	رُسُلٌ	عَمَلٌ	مَرَضٌ	بَلَدٍ
نَهَرٍ	قَسَمٌ	لَعِبًا	رَهَقًا	هُزُوًا
رَصَدًا	عَلَقٍ	أُذُنٌ	لَعِبٌ	أَجَلٌ
أُكُلٍ	سُرُرٌ	شَجَرٌ	ثَمَنًا	ظَمَأً
رَشَدًا	سَفَرٍ	قَدَمٌ	كُتُبٌ	غَضَبٍ
غَبَرَةٌ	عَلَقَةٍ	كَبِدٍ	حَكَمًا	سُقُفًا
دَرَجَةٌ	حَسَنَةٌ	بَقَرَةٌ	شَجَرَةٌ	قَتَرَةٌ

- Read and spell all the words **fluently** with their correct pronunciation.
- Read an **entire line** without taking a breath or pausing.

- Read in a random order, pointing at random words, reading them as quickly as possible.
- Practice one word at a time until you have read a whole line. Then try to say it all in one go.

- I can **read and spell** all the words **quickly**.
- I can read an **entire line** without pausing.
- I can implement all the lessons learnt previously into this exercise.

GRADE 05

The Prophet ﷺ said:

"The one who was devoted to the Qur'an will be told on the Day of Resurrection: 'Recite and ascend (in ranks) as you used to recite when you were in the world. Your rank will be at the last Ayah you recite."

(Abu Dawood and Tirmidhi)

OVERVIEW

LESSON 09 — FAT-HAH FOLLOWED BY AN ALIF

- Fat-hah followed by an Alif is a stretched Fat-hah.
- A letter with a Fat-hah followed by an empty Alif without a Harakah (symbol) above it will be stretched to double the stretch of a Fat-hah (1 second).

LESSON 10 — MADD FAT-HAH

- Madd Fat-hah is a stretched Fat-hah.
- A letter with a Madd Fat-hah will be stretched to double the stretch of a Fat-hah (1 second).

LESSON 11 — MADD KASRAH

- Madd Kasrah is a stretched Kasrah.
- A letter with a Madd Kasrah will be stretched to double the stretch of a Kasrah (1 second).

LESSON 12 — MADD DHAMMAH

- Madd Dhammah is a stretched Dhammah.
- A letter with a Madd Dhammah will be stretched to double the stretch of a Dhammah (1 second).

Extension = More practice before progressing further.

LESSON 09 — FAT-HAH FOLLOWED BY AN ALIF

| بَا | تَا | ثَا | جَا | حَا | خَا | دَا | ذَا | رَا | زَا |

| سَا | شَا | صَا | ضَا | طَا | ظَا | عَا | غَا | فَا | قَا |

| كَا | لَا | مَا | نَا | وَا | هَا | ئَا | يَا |

EXERCISE

| ذَاتَ | خَافَ | كَانَ | تَابَ | نَارًا |

| هَادِ | عَابِدٌ | نَبَاتَ | حَافِظُ | ثُبَاتِ |

| جُنَاَة | كَاتِبٌ | مَالِكُ | غَاسِقٍ | ثَوَابًا |

| جَاعِلٌ | دَابِرَ | صَوَابًا | آفَاقَ | خَالِدًا |

| وَلَعَلَا | مُطَاعٍ | أَصَابَ | يَخَافُ | كَوَاعِبَ |

STEP BY STEP

•▶ Read the letters that have an Alif.
E.g. Baa بَا , Taa تَا , Thaa ثَا .

•▶ Spell the letters that have an Alif.
E.g. Ba, Alif Fat-hah = Baa. Ta, Alif Fat-hah = Taa.
Tha, Alif, Fat-hah = Thaa.

•▶ Read the words without spelling.
E.g. Thaa-ta, Khaa-fa, Kaa-na.

•▶ Spell the words. E.g.

Step 1	Thaal, Alif Fat-hah = Thaa	ذَا
Step 2	Ta, Fat-hah = Ta	تَ
Step 3	Read the entire word, Thaa-Ta	ذَاتَ

Read the letter **Ra** as a **Full Mouth Letter** when it has a Fat-hah and an Alif.

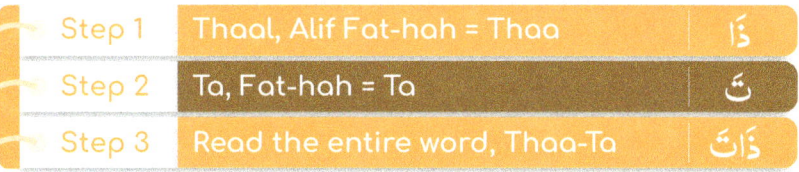

•▶ If an empty Alif comes after a Fat-hah letter, it will be stretched twice the length of a Fat-hah.

•▶ As soon as you point at a word you should be able to read it straight away.

QUICK TIPS

CHECKLIST

☺ I can read and spell words which have **Fat-hah and Alif** fluently.

☺ I can read  as a **Full Mouth Letter** when it comes with a Fat-hah and Alif.

☺ I can read each line fluently in one breath (without hesitation or pausing).

61 Comments

LESSON 09: SINGLE AND DUAL WORDS

بَا

فَوَاكِهَ	زَالَتَا	زَاهِقٌ	سَأَلَهَا	أَسَاوِرَ
بِوَلَدِهَا	دَافِقٍ	مَوَاخِرَ	هَامِدَةً	تَظَاهَرَا
مُتَشَابِهٍ	عَلَانِيَةً	فَتَطَاوَلَ	سُرَادِقُهَا	مُتَرَاكِبًا

فَلَا جُنَاحَ	فَلَا تُمَارِ	وَلَا حَامٍ
لَا طَاقَةَ لَنَا	نَارًا أَحَاطَ	مَا وَعَدَنَا
أَصَابَهَا وَابِلٌ	كَانَ مِزَاجُهَا	كَانَ فَاسِقًا
غِلَاظٌ شِدَادٌ	تِجَارَةً حَاضِرَةً	سَحَابًا ثِقَالًا
عَدَسِهَا وَبَصَلِهَا	عَالِيَهَا سَافِلَهَا	طَعَامُكَ وَشَرَابِكَ
وَلَا تَزِرُ وَازِرَةٌ	بَابًا ذَا عَذَابٍ	لِبَاسَهُمَا لِيُرِيَهُمَا

- Read and spell the single and dual words that have **Fat-hah followed by an Alif**.
- Read the dual and plural words **quickly and properly without pausing**.
- Read each line without stopping after the words.

Look at all the symbols carefully, remember not to stretch the Fat-hah, Kasrah and Dhammah letters.

- I can **read and spell** the letters and words **quickly and fluently**.
- I can read each line **fluently in one breath** (without hesitation or pausing).
- I can implement all the lessons learnt previously into this exercise.

LESSON 10: MADD FAT-HAH

اْ	بْ	تْ	ثْ	جْ	حْ	خْ	دْ	ذْ	رْ

زْ	سْ	شْ	صْ	ضْ	طْ	ظْ	عْ	غْ	فْ

قْ	كْ	لْ	مْ	نْ	وْ	هْ	ءْ	ىْ

EXERCISE

اِلَه	اٰيِتِ	رَاُه	اخَ	اٰدَمَ

اٰمَنَ	اٰتهُ	تُرْبًا	مَاٰبًا	عِظَاٰمًا

كِلْهُمَا	سُلَلَةٍ	فَتَبٰرَكَ	شِبْخِتِ	قِصٰرتٌ

يُصْلِحُ	شَنَاٰنُ	تَزٰوَرُ	اٰمِنَةً	كٰشِفَتُ

خٰلِتِكَ	رِسٰلتِ	قُنِتُّ	حٰفِظْتُ	مُتَجٰوِرٰتٌ

   Completed on ___ / ___ / ___

STEP BY STEP

• Read the letters that have a Madd Fat-hah.
  E.g. Aa ﺍ, Baa ﺑﺎ, Taa ﺗﺎ.

• Spell the letters. E.g. Alif, Madd Fat-hah = Aa. Ba, Madd Fat-hah = Baa. Ta, Madd-Fat-hah = Taa.

• Read the words without spelling.
  E.g. E-laa-ha, Aa-yaa-te, Ra-aa-hu.

• Spell the words. E.g.

Step 1	Alif, Kasrah = E	ﺍ
Step 2	Laam, Madd Fat-hah = Laa	ﻻ
Step 3	Join the two, E-laa	ﺇﻻ
Step 4	Ha, Fat-hah = Ha	ﻪ
Step 5	Read the entire word, E-Laa-Ha	ﺇﻟٰﻪ

Read the letter **Ra as a Full Mouth Letter** when it has a Madd Fat-hah.

QUICK TIPS

• Stretch the Madd Fat-hah twice the length of a Fat-hah (1 second).

• As soon as you point at a word you should be able to read it straight away.

CHECKLIST

☑ I can **read and spell** the words which have **Madd Fat-hah** fluently.

☑ I can read ﺭ as a **Full Mouth Letter** when it comes with a Madd Fat-hah.

☑ I can read each line **fluently in one breath** (without hesitation or pausing).

LESSON 11 — MADD KASRAH

ا ب ت ث ج ح خ د ذ ر

ز س ش ص ض ط ظ ع غ ف

ق ك ل م ن و ه ء ي

EXERCISE

اِلِفِ هَـٰذِهِ وَلَدِهِ عَقِبِهِ بِيَدِهِ

اٰيتِهِ عَمِلِهِ قِبَلِهِ ثَمَرِهِ عُنُقِهِ

اَجَلِهِ عُمُرِهِ وَالِدِهِ بَصَرِهِ وَرُسُلِهِ

عِبَادِهِ طَعَامِهِ جِهَادِهِ رِسلِتِهِ نِعَاجِهِ

تِلَاوَتِهِ شَاكِلَتِهِ بِشِمَالِهِ مَوَاضِعِهِ نَابِجَانِبِهِ

STEP BY STEP

- Read the letters that have a Madd Kasrah.
  E.g. Ee إ, Bee بِ, Tee تِ.

- Spell the letters that have a Madd Kasrah.
  E.g. Alif, Madd Kasrah = Ee. Ba, Madd Kasrah = Bee. Ta Madd kasrah = Tee.

- Read the words without spelling.
  E.g. Ee-laa-fe, Haa-The-hee, Wa-la-de-hee.

- Spell the words. E.g.

Step 1	Alif, Madd Kasrah = Ee	إ
Step 2	Laam, Madd Fat-ha = Laa	لَ
Step 3	Join the letters, Ee-Laa	إلَ
Step 4	Fa, Kasrah = Fe	فِ
Step 5	Read the entire word, Ee-Laa-Fe	إلَفِ

QUICK TIPS

- Stretch the Madd Kasrah twice the length of a Kasrah (1 second).

- As soon as you point at a word you should be able to read it straight away.

CHECKLIST

- ✓ I can **read and spell** the words which have **Madd Kasrah** fluently.

- ✓ I can read each line **fluently in one breath** (without hesitation or pausing).

- ✓ I can implement all the lessons learnt previously into this exercise.

LESSON 12: MADD DHAMMAH

اُ بُ تُ ثُ جُ حُ خُ دُ ذُ رُ

زُ سُ شُ صُ ضُ طُ ظُ عُ غُ فُ

قُ كُ لُ مُ نُ وُ هُ ءُ ىُ

EXERCISE

فَعَلَهُ سَمِعَهُ مَلَأَهُ اَمَرَهُ رُسُلَهُ

خِثْمُهُ اَجَلَهُ قَدَرُهُ وَثَاقَهُ ظِلُّهُ

فَتَرَكَهُ فِظْلُهُ بَيَانَهُ وَزَادَهُ خُمُسَهُ

بَرَكْتُهُ اَمَانَتَهُ حِسَابَهُ فَاَمَاتَهُ صَلَاتَهُ

وَبَاطِنَهُ يُحَاوِرُهُ فَاَصَابَهُ مَفَاتِحَهُ فَيُضْعِفُهُ

STEP BY STEP

- Read the letters that have a Madd Dhammah.
  E.g. Oo ﺃُ, Boo ﺑُ, Too ﺗُ.

- Spell the letters that have Madd Dhammah.
  E.g. Alif, Madd Fat-hah = Oo. Ba, Madd Dhammah = Boo. Ta, Madd Dhammah = Too.

- Spell the words. E.g.

Step 1	Fa, Fat-hah = Fa	فَ
Step 2	'Ayn, Fat-hah = 'A	عَ
Step 3	Join the letters, Fa-'A	فَعَ
Step 4	Laam, Fat-hah = La	لَ
Step 5	Join the letters, Fa-'A-la	فَعَلَ
Step 6	Ha, Madd Dhammah = Hoo	هُ
Step 7	Read the entire word, Fa-'A-la-hoo	فَعَلَهُ

QUICK TIPS

- Stretch the Madd Dhammah twice the length of a Dhammah (1 second).

- As soon as you point at a word you should be able to read it straight away.

CHECKLIST

- I can **read and spell** the words which have **Madd Dhammah** fluently.

- I can read each line **fluently in one breath** (without hesitation or pausing).

- I can implement all the lessons learnt previously into this exercise.

EXERCISE 09-12 — EXTENSION

فَاٰمَنَ لَهٗ	اِلٰهَهٗ هَوٰهُ	اٰلَ دَاوٗدَ
لَهٗ وَلَدٌ	مَعَهٗۤ اَخَاهُ	اِلٰهً اٰخَرَ
لَا عِوَجَ لَهٗ	هٰذِهٖ نَاقَةٌ	ذٰلِكَ لَاٰيَةً

وَمَا كَانَ لَهٗ	تَابَ وَاٰمَنَ	ذٰلِكَ قِوَامًا
هٰذَا اٰبَاِلِهَتِنَا	هٰذَا السِّحْرُ	ثَالِثُ ثَلٰثَةٍ
خَلَقَهٗ وَبَدَاَ	فَصِيَامُ ثَلٰثَةٍ	كَانَ بِعِبَادِهٖ

هٰذَا مَا وَعَدَنَا	وَثُلُثَ وَرُبُعَ	لَجَعَلَهٗ سَاكِنًا
اِذَا جَعَلَهٗ نَارًا	مَالُهٗ وَوَلَدُهٗ	وَكَانَ لَهٗ ثَمَرٌ
لَقِيَا غُلٰمًا قَتَلَهٗ	عَمِلَهٖ فَاَحْسَنَا	فَاِذَا اَصَابَ بِهٖ

  Completed on / /

70

STEP BY STEP

- ▸ Read and spell the dual and plural words that include all previous Harakaat on them fluently:
  - Fat-hah, Kasrah and Dhammah
  - Fat-ha-tayn, Kasra-tayn and Dhamma-tayn
  - Fat-hah letters followed by an empty Alif
  - Madd Fat-hah, Madd Kasrah and Madd Dhammah

- ▸ Read the **dual and plural words** quickly and properly without pausing.

- ▸ Read each line **without stopping** after the words.

QUICK TIPS

- ▸ Only stretch the letter that has a Fat-hah and Alif, Madd Fat-hah, Madd Kasrah and Madd Dhammah.

- ▸ The letter Ra will read with an empty mouth when comes with a Kasrah or Madd Kasrah, otherwise it will always be read with a full mouth.

CHECKLIST

- ✓ I can **read and spell** the letters and words fluently.
- ✓ I can read each line **fluently in one breath** (without hesitation or pausing).
- ✓ I can implement all the lessons learnt previously into this exercise.

Comments

GRADE 06

The Prophet ﷺ said:

"Read the Qur'aan, for it will come as an intercessor for its reciters on the Day of Resurrection."

(Muslim)

OVERVIEW

LESSON 13 > **SUKOON**

- A letter with a **Sukoon** اَنْ on it indicates that the sound of the letter before it will be joining onto it.
The letter that has a Sukoon on it is known as a **Saakin** letter.

EXERCISE 01 SUKOON IN SINGLE AND DUAL WORDS

- Students should be able to **identify** and **read** all the words that have a **Sukoon** or **multiple Sukoon's** in them.

Note: An empty Alif ا or an Alif that comes after a Kasrah will be cancelled.

Lesson 13: SUKOON

مِنْ	بَلْ	اَمْ	اِذْ	اَنْ
دَعْ	عِدْ	سَلْ	عَنْ	قُلْ
كُلْ	قَدْ	ذُقْ	هَبْ	خُنْ
يَتُبْ	مِثْلَ	لَحْمَ	فَصْلُ	اَتَتْ
كُرْهًا	اِثْمٌ	اَمْرٍ	سِحْرٌ	رِزْقٍ
نَقْعًا	طَلْعٌ	بَعْضَ	نَخْلٍ	نَحْسٍ
بَلْدَةً	اَلْقٰى	كَلْمَحِ	تَنْزِعُ	فَضْلًا
تَرَكْنَا	طَعْمُهٗ	شَطْاَهٗ	اَقْبَلَ	غَمْرَةٍ
قَسَمْنَا	تَبْصِرَةً	نِعْمَةً	تَحْبَطْ	اَظْلَمَ

Completed on D D / M M / YEAR

- ▸ Read the words that have a Sukoon.
  E.g. An اَنْ, Idh اِذْ, Am اَمْ.

- ▸ Spell the words. E.g.

 Alif, Noon, Fat-hah = An

When you see a letter with a Sukoon اَنْ, join it to the letter before.

- ✓ I can **read and spell** the Saakin letters and words.
- ✓ I can read each line **fluently in one breath** (without hesitation or pausing).
- ✓ I can implement all the lessons learnt previously into this exercise.

EXERCISE 01 — SUKOON IN SINGLE AND DUAL WORDS

اَضْحَكَ	قُرْبَانًا	مَغْفِرَةً	اَنْزَلَ	بَعْضًا
مُنْتَشِرٌ	اَثَابَهُمْ	مُسْتَطَرٌ	مُقْتَدِرٍ	مُحْتَظِرٍ
اَنْتُمْ	مُنْتَصِرٌ	صَرْصَرًا	لِتَسْتَوُوا	تَنْتَصِرَانِ
بَعْضُهُمْ	يُجِرْكُمْ	فَعَلْتُمْ	اِفْكُهُمْ	يَبْخَلْ
اَعْمَالَهُمْ	تُصِبْكُمْ	رِزْقُكُمْ	ظَنَنْتُمْ	اَعْتَدْنَا
اَبْصَارُهُمْ	اَرْسَلْنٰكَ	اَرْحَامَكُمْ	فِتْنَتَكُمْ	اَنْفُسِكُمْ

وَنَحْنُ اَقْرَبُ	مِنْهُمْ بَطْشًا	بَعْدَ ظُلْمِهٖ
تَوَارَتْ بِالْحِجَابِ	اَسْتَجِبْ لَكُمْ	سَمْعِهٖ وَقَلْبِهٖ

- ▸ Read and spell the words that include two Saakin letters in one word fluently.
- ▸ Read and spell the **double words** confidently and fluently. E.g.

Step 1	Ba, 'Ayn, Fat-hah = Ba'	بَعْ
Step 2	Dhaad, Fat-ha-tayn = Dhan	ضًا
Step 3	Read the entire word, Ba'-Dhan	بَعْضًا

Remember, it is a quick join!

QUICK TIPS

- ✓ I can **read and spell** the dual Saakin letters and words.
- ✓ I can read each line **fluently in one breath** (without hesitation or pausing).
- ✓ I can implement all the lessons learnt previously into this exercise.

Comments

GRADE 07

The Prophet ﷺ said:

"Read the Qur'aan regularly. By the One in Whose Hand Muhammad's soul is, it escapes from memory faster than a camel does from its tying ropes."

(Muslim)

OVERVIEW

LESSON 14 — **FAT-HAH FOLLOWED BY A 'WAW' SAAKIN**

- When a Waw Saakin comes after a letter with a Fat-hah أَوْ , the letter will be read **without a stretch.**

Note: When a Waw Saakin comes after a letter with a Fat-hah at the end of a word, it will have an empty Alif which is silent and will be ignored.

LESSON 15 — **DHAMMAH FOLLOWED BY A 'WAW' SAAKIN**

- When a Waw Saakin comes after a letter with a Dhammah أُوْ , the **letter will be stretched** for a second or so.

- The stretch will be similar to Madd Dhammah.

Note: When a Waw Saakin comes after a letter with a Dhammah at the end of a word, it will have an empty Alif which is silent and will be ignored.

EXERCISE 01   DUAL WORDS

The student must be confident in reading the bigger words that include Fat-hah/Dhammah followed by Waw Saakin. These words will give them the practice they need so when they progress they know where to apply the stretch and where not to.

LESSON 14

FAT-HAH FOLLOWED BY A ' WAW ' SAAKIN

أَوْ

اَوْ بَوْ جَوْ حَوْ خَوْ دَوْ ذَوْ رَوْ

زَوْ سَوْ شَوْ صَوْ ضَوْ طَوْ ظَوْ عَوْ غَوْ فَوْ

قَوْ كَوْ لَوْ مَوْ نَوْ وَوْ هَوْ ءَوْ يَوْ

EXERCISE

رَوْحٌ	غَوْرًا	سَوْفَ	زَوْجًا	يَرَوْا
لَوْحٍ	صَوْمًا	سَوْطٌ	خَلَوْا	عَصَوْا
عَفَوْنَا	حَوْلَهُ	تَوْبَةٌ	مَوْتِهَا	كَوْكَبًا
غَدَوْتَ	قَوْمُكَ	بِعَوْرَةٍ	مَوْعِدُهُ	يَنْهَوْنَ
تَنْسَوْنَ	مَوْلٰهُمْ	يُجْزَوْنَ	أَوْلَادُهُمْ	مُسْتَوْدَعٌ

    Completed on

- Read the small words without spelling.
  E.g. Aw أَوْ, Baw بَوْ, Taw تَوْ.

- Spell the small words that include a Fat-hah followed by a Waw Saakin.
  E.g. Alif, Waw, Fat-hah = Aw. Ba, Waw, Fat-hah = Baw. Ta, Waw, Fat-hah = Taw.

- Read the words. E.g. Rawhoon, Ghawran, Sawfa.

- Spell the words. E.g.

Step 1	Ra, Waw, Fat-hah = Raw	رَوْ
Step 2	Ha, Dhamma-tayn = Hoon	هٌ
Step 3	Read the entire word, Raw-Hoon	رَوْهٌ

QUICK TIPS

When Fat-hah is joining onto Waw Saakin أَوْ, don't stretch the sound of the Fat-hah letter.

E.g. Fat-hah followed by Waw Saakin = Aw.

- I can **read and spell** the **Fat-hah followed by a Waw Saakin**.

- I can read each line **fluently in one breath** (without hesitation or pausing).

- I can implement all the lessons learnt previously into this exercise.

LESSON 15: DHAMMAH FOLLOWED BY A 'WAW' SAAKIN

اُوْ

اُوْ   بُوْ   تُوْ   ثُوْ   جُوْ   حُوْ   خُوْ   دُوْ   ذُوْ   رُوْ

زُوْ   سُوْ   شُوْ   صُوْ   ضُوْ   طُوْ   ظُوْ   عُوْ   غُوْ   فُوْ

قُوْ   كُوْ   لُوْ   مُوْ   نُوْ   وُوْ   هُوْ   ءُوْ   يُوْ

EXERCISE

قَالُوْا   أَوْفُوْا   فَعَلُوْا   أَوْقَدُوْا   تَكُوْنُوْا

سَارِعُوْا   مَوْفُوْرًا   مَوْزُوْنٍ   نَتْلُوْهَا   يَخَافُوْا

تَصْبِرُوْا   خَسِرُوْا   يَرْجِعُوْنَ   يَعْرِفُوْنَهُ   مَغْلُوْلَةٌ

يُخْدِعُوْنَ   تُرْحَمُوْنَ   وَاعْتَصِمُوْا   يَفْقَهُوْهُ   وَاخْتَلَفُوْا

مُتْرَفُوْهَا   يَعْتَدُوْنَ   فَيَنْقَلِبُوْا   مُتَقَبِّلُوْنَ   تَلْبِسُوْنَهَا

STEP BY STEP

- Read the small words without spelling.
  E.g. Oo اُو , Boo بُو , Too تُو .

- Spell the small words that include a Dhammah followed by a Waw Saakin.
  E.g. Alif, Waw, Dhammah = Oo. Ba, Waw, Dhammah = Boo. Ta, Waw, Dhammah = Too.

- Read the words. E.g. Qaaloo, Awfoo, Fa'aloo.

- Spell the words. E.g.

Step 1	Qaaf, Alif, Fat-hah = Qaa	قَا
Step 2	Laam, Waw, Dhammah = Loo	لُوْا
Step 3	Read the whole word, Qaa-Loo	قَالُوْا

QUICK TIPS

When a Dhammah is joining onto a Waw Saakin اُوْ , stretch the sound of the Dhammah letter for around a second or so.

E.g. Dhammah followed by Waw Saakin = Oo.

CHECKLIST

- I can read and spell the **Dhammah followed by a Waw Saakin.**
- I can read each line **fluently in one breath** (without hesitation or pausing).
- I can implement all the lessons learnt previously into this exercise.

EXERCISE 01 — DUAL WORDS

يٰقَوْمِ اذْكُرُوْا	وَلْيَقُوْلُوْا قَوْلًا	وَقَوْلِهِمْ قُلُوْبُنَا
تَعَالَوْا قَاتِلُوْا	وَاكْسُوْهُمْ وَقُوْلُوْا	فَسَوْفَ تَعْلَمُوْنَ
وَرَفَعْنَا فَوْقَهُمْ	يُقَاتِلُوْا قَوْمَهُمْ	أَوْ تُخْفُوْهُ أَوْ تَعْفُوْا
وَسَوْفَ تُسْـَٔلُوْنَ	أَوِ الْخَوْفِ أَذَاعُوْا	هَاجَرُوْا وَأُخْرِجُوْا
وَلَا تَهِنُوْا وَلَا تَحْزَنُوْا	وَأَصْلَحُوْا وَاعْتَصَمُوْا	وَقَعَدُوْا لَوْ أَطَاعُوْنَا
قٰتَلُوْكُمْ فَاقْتُلُوْهُمْ	أَوْسَطِ مَا تُطْعِمُوْنَ	وَرَسُوْلَهٗ وَيَسْعَوْنَ
وَصَابِرُوْا وَرَابِطُوْا	نُشُوْزًا أَوْ إِعْرَاضًا	ثَقِفْتُمُوْهُمْ وَأَخْرِجُوْهُمْ
جَمَعُوْا لَكُمْ فَاخْشَوْهُمْ	فَلَا تَخْشَوْهُمْ وَاخْشَوْنِ	ظُهُوْرِهِمْ وَاشْتَرَوْا بِهٖ

Completed on   /   /

STEP BY STEP

➤ Spell the words. E.g.

Step 1	Ya, Madd, Fat-hah = Yaa	يَا
Step 2	Qaaf, Waw, Fat-hah = Qaw	قَوْ
Step 3	Join the two letters, Yaa-Qaw	يَقَوْ
Step 4	Meem, Thaal, Kasrah = Mith	مِذ
Step 5	Join all previous, Yaa-Qaw-Mith	يَقَوْمِذ
Step 6	Kaaf Dhammah = Ku	كُ
Step 7	Join all previous, Yaa-Qaw-Mith-Ku	يَقَوْمِذْكُ
Step 8	Ra, Waw, Dhammah = Roo	رُوْ
Step 9	Read the entire word, Yaa-Qaw-Mith-Ku-Roo	يَقَوْمِذْكُرُوْا

QUICK TIPS

➤ Fat-hah joining onto a Waw أَوْ = **No stretch**

➤ Dhammah joining onto a Waw أُوْ = **Stretch**

CHECKLIST

☑ I can **read and spell** the words that have a **Waw Saakin** fluently.

☑ I can read each line **fluently in one breath** (without hesitation or pausing).

☑ I can implement all the lessons learnt previously into this exercise.

GRADE 08

The Prophet ﷺ said:

"Read the Qur'aan, for it will come as an intercessor for its reciters on the Day of Resurrection."

(Muslim)

OVERVIEW

LESSON 16 — **FAT-HAH FOLLOWED BY A 'YA' SAAKIN**

- When a Ya Saakin comes after a letter with a Fat-hah اَيْ , the letter will be read **without a stretch**..

LESSON 17 — **KASRAH FOLLOWED BY A 'YA' SAAKIN**

- When a Ya Saakin comes after a letter with a Kasrah اِيْ , the **letter will be stretched** for a second or so.

- The stretch will be similar to Madd Kasrah.

EXERCISE 01 — DUAL AND PLURAL WORDS

The student must be confident in reading the bigger words that include Fat-hah/Kasrah followed by Ya Saakin. These words will give them the practice they need so when they move on they know where to apply the stretch and where not to.

EXERCISE 02 — SHORT VERSE FLUENCY

The student will get a feel of the bigger words and sentences as they appear in the Qur'aan.
The teacher should take a mini test at this stage before progressing to the next grade. If the student is applying all the rules properly and reading fluently then they should move on. If not, revision is required until they are fluent.
This will give them extra practice and boost their confidence.

LESSON 16: FAT-HAH FOLLOWED BY A 'YA' SAAKIN — اَىْ

اَىْ بَىْ تَىْ ثَىْ جَىْ حَىْ خَىْ دَىْ ذَىْ رَىْ

زَىْ سَىْ شَىْ صَىْ ضَىْ طَىْ ظَىْ عَىْ غَىْ فَىْ

قَىْ كَىْ لَىْ مَىْ نَىْ وَىْ هَىْ أَىْ يَىْ

EXERCISE

مَيْتًا طَيْرًا رَأَيْتَ رُوَيْدًا بَيْتِهٖ

فَأَبَيْنَ ذَوَاتَيْ صَيْحَةً قَضَيْنَا أَبَوَيْهِ

كَهَيْئَةِ عَقِبَيْهِ حَيْرَانَ اِلَهَيْنِ أَوْدَيْنِ

شَفَتَيْنِ زَوْجَيْنِ وَهَدَيْنَٰهُمْ فَأَحْيَيْنَهُ فَتَعَالَيْنَ

بِالْوَالِدَيْنِ لَهَدَيْنَٰهُمْ وَاجْتَبَيْنَٰهُمْ فَأَغْوَيْنٰكُمْ فَأَغْشَيْنَٰهُمْ

STEP BY STEP

• ▶ Read the small words without spelling.
E.g. Ay أَيْ, Bay بَيْ, Tay تَيْ.

• ▶ Spell the small words that include a Fat-hah followed by a 'Ya' Saakin.
E.g. Alif, Ya, Fat-hah = Ay. Ba, Ya, Fat-hah = Bay. Ta, Ya, Fat-hah = Tay.

• ▶ Read the words. E.g. Maytan, Tayran, Ra-'ayta.

• ▶ Spell the words. E.g.

Step 1	Meem, Ya, Fat-hah = May	مَيْ
Step 2	Ta, Fat-ha-tayn = Tan	تًا
Step 3	Read the whole word, May-Tan	مَيْتًا

When Fat-hah is joining onto a Ya Saakin أَيْ, don't stretch the sound of the Fat-hah letter.

E.g. Fat-hah followed by Ya Saakin = Ay.

QUICK TIPS

CHECKLIST

☾ I can **read and spell** the Fat-hah followed by a Ya Saakin.

☾ I can read each line **fluently in one breath** (without hesitation or pausing).

☾ I can implement all the lessons learnt previously into this exercise.

LESSON 17 — KASRAH FOLLOWED BY A 'YA' SAAKIN

اِیْ بِیْ تِیْ ثِیْ جِیْ حِیْ خِیْ دِیْ ذِیْ رِیْ

زِیْ سِیْ شِیْ صِیْ ضِیْ طِیْ ظِیْ عِیْ غِیْ فِیْ

قِیْ کِیْ لِیْ مِیْ نِیْ وِیْ هِیْ ئِیْ يِیْ

EXERCISE

اَبْغِیْ سَلِیْم اَثِیْمًا دِیْنًا بَنِیْنَ

طٰغِیْنَ لَیَبْغِیْ اَقِیْمُوْا اَرُوْنِیْ شِیْعَتِه

سَیُصِیْبُ تَبْدِیْلًا مُقْنِعِیْ یٰلَیْتَنِیْ مُدْبِرِیْنَ

غَرَابِیْبُ مِسْکِیْنًا مُهْطِعِیْنَ تُصْحِبْنِیْ یُطِیْقُوْنَهٗ

مُعْرِضِیْنَ لِتَسْتَبِیْنَ سَرَابِیْلُهُمْ بِمَبْعُوْثِیْنَ سَیَجْزِیْهِمْ

STEP BY STEP

- ▸ Read the small words without spelling.
  E.g. Ee إِي, Bee بِي, Tee تِي.

- ▸ Spell the small words that include a Kasrah followed by a 'Ya' Saakin. E.g. Alif, Ya, Kasrah = Ee. Ba, Ya, Kasrah = Bee. Ta, Ya, Kasrah = Tee.

- ▸ Read the words.
  E.g. Ab-ghee, Salee-min, Athee-man.

- ▸ Spell the words. E.g.

Step 1	Alif, Ba, Fat-hah = Ab	اَبْ
Step 2	Ghayn, Ya, Kasrah = Ghee	غِي
Step 3	Read the whole word, Ab-Ghee	اَبْغِي

QUICK TIPS

When a Kasrah is joining onto a Ya Saakin إِي , stretch the sound of the Kasrah letter for around a second or so.

E.g. Kasrah followed by Ya Saakin = Eee.

CHECKLIST

- ✓ I can **read and spell** the Kasrah followed by a Ya Saakin.

- ✓ I can read each line **fluently in one breath** (without hesitation or pausing).

- ✓ I can implement all the lessons learnt previously into this exercise.

EXERCISE 01 — DUAL AND PLURAL WORDS

خَيْرًا كَثِيرًا	اِبْرَاهِيمَ خَلِيلًا	وَأَكِيدُ كَيْدًا
عَلَيْكَ عَظِيمًا	عَلَيْهِمْ شَهِيدًا	صَلَاتِي وَنُسُكِي
اِلَيْهِمْ خٰشِعِينَ	وَمُهَيْمِنًا عَلَيْهِ	خٰلِدِينَ فِيهَا
رَأَيْتَ الْمُنٰفِقِينَ	غَيْرَ مُسَافِحِينَ	عَلَيْكُمْ نِعْمَتِي
مَقَامِي وَتَذْكِيرِي	فَلَمَسُوهُ بِأَيْدِيهِمْ	غَيْرَ مَعْرُوشٰتٍ
بِوُجُوهِكُمْ وَأَيْدِيكُمْ	فَاشْهَدُوا عَلَيْهِمْ	فَتَنْقَلِبُوا خٰسِرِينَ
وَارْزُقُوهُمْ فِيهَا	وَلَا يُظْلَمُونَ نَقِيرًا	وَأُوذُوا فِي سَبِيلِي
كَانَ عَلَيْكُمْ رَقِيبًا	أُجُورَكُمْ يَوْمَ الْقِيٰمَةِ	مُذَبْذَبِينَ بَيْنَ ذٰلِكَ
فَأَفُوزَ فَوْزًا عَظِيمًا	نُمْلِي لَهُمْ لِيَزْدَادُوا	وَاتْلُ عَلَيْهِمْ نَبَأَ ابْنَيْ

STEP BY STEP

•▶ Spell the words. E.g.

Step 1	Kha, Ya, Fat-hah = Khay	خَيْ
Step 2	Ra, Fat-ha-tayn = Ran	رًا
Step 3	Join the two letters, Khay-Ran	خَيْرًا
Step 4	Kaaf, Fat-hah = Ka	كَ
Step 5	Join all previous, Khay-Ran-Ka	خَيْرًا كَ
Step 6	Tha, Ya, Kasrah = Thee	ثِيْ
Step 7	Join all previous, Khay-Ran-Ka-Thee	خَيْرًا كَثِيْ
Step 8	Ra, Fat-ha-tayn = Ran	رًا
Step 9	Read the entire word, Khay-Ran-Ka-Thee-Ran	خَيْرًا كَثِيْرًا

QUICK TIPS

•▶ Fat-hah joining onto a Waw اَوْ , or Fat-hah joining a Ya اَيْ = **No stretch**
•▶ Dhammah joining onto a Waw اُوْ , or Kasrah joining onto a Ya اِيْ = **Stretch**

CHECKLIST

☑ I **can read and spell** the words that have a Ya Saakin fluently.

☑ I can read each line **fluently in one breath** (without hesitation or pausing).

☑ I can implement all the lessons learnt previously into this exercise.

EXERCISE 02 — SHORT VERSE FLUENCY

اَنْ تَمِیْلُوْا مَیْلًا عَظِیْمًا	وَجَدَ عِنْدَهَا رِزْقًا
وَخُلِقَ الْاِنْسَانُ ضَعِیْفًا	قَدْ اَنْزَلْنَا عَلَیْكُمْ لِبَاسًا
وَمَا جَعَلْنٰكَ عَلَیْهِمْ حَفِیْظًا	لِمَ تَقُوْلُوْنَ مَا لَا تَفْعَلُوْنَ
یُصْهَرُ بِهٖ مَا فِیْ بُطُوْنِهِمْ	فَمَنْ اَبْصَرَ فَلِنَفْسِهٖ
وَهُوَ اَعْلَمُ بِالْمُهْتَدِیْنَ	مَنْ اَرْسَلْنَا عَلَیْهِ حَاصِبًا

لِمَ تَعْبُدُ مَا لَا یَسْمَعُ وَلَا یُبْصِرُ وَلَا یُغْنِیْ عَنْكَ شَیْئًا

فَمَنْ اٰمَنَ وَاَصْلَحَ فَلَا خَوْفٌ عَلَیْهِمْ وَلَا هُمْ یَحْزَنُوْنَ

لَئِنْ اُخْرِجُوْا لَا یَخْرُجُوْنَ مَعَهُمْ وَلَئِنْ قُوْتِلُوْا لَا یَنْصُرُوْنَهُمْ

- ▸ Read and spell the small sentences.
- ▸ Apply the **stretch on the correct letters**.
- ▸ Read an entire sentence without pausing or hesitation.

- ▸ If an empty Alif comes between two words وَخُلِقَ اْلاِنْسَانُ , it will be ignored.
- ▸ Split the big words into smaller chunks, and read them efficiently before reading the whole word.

- ⓒ I can **read and spell** the **sentences** correctly and fluently.
- ⓒ I can read each **sentence in one breath** (without hesitation or pausing).
- ⓒ I can implement all the lessons learnt previously into this exercise.

Comments

GRADE 09

The Prophet ﷺ said:
"Whoever recites a letter from the Book of Allaah, he will be credited with a good deed, and a good deed gets a ten-fold reward. I do not say that Alif-Laam-Meem is one letter, but Alif is a letter, Laam is a letter and Meem is a letter."
(Muslim)

OVERVIEW

LESSON 18 > **SHADDAH STRONG JOIN**

The Shaddah  represents the merging of two letters, one with a Sukoon and the other with a Harakah: رَ + بْ = رَبَّ
Listen to the student carefully so that they are pronouncing the strong join properly.
The student should be confident and fluent in reading with spelling and without spelling.

EXERCISE 01 — Double Shaddah words

The student must be confident in reading Shaddah letters properly when appearing in bigger words: وَالرُّمَّانَ
Listen to the student carefully so that they are pronouncing all the strong joins properly.
Always listen to the student read without spelling first, and then ask the student to spell random words so you are able to assess their progress accurately.

If an empty Alif ا comes in the middle of a word it will be cancelled.

EXERCISE 02 & 03 — Dual words (Consecutive strong joins)

The student must be confident in reading Shaddah letters when written in dual and plural words: وَكَلَّمَ اللهُ
Listen to the student carefully so that they are pronouncing all the strong joins properly.
Always listen to the student read without spelling first, and then ask the student to spell random words so you are able to assess their progress accurately.

If an empty Alif ا comes in the middle of a word it will be cancelled.

LESSON 18 — SHADDAH

رَبْ + بَ = رَبَّ   قَلْ + لَ = قَلَّ   اَنْ + نَ = اَنَّ

اِنَّ ثُمَّ عَمَّ مَنْ مَدَّ حَجَّ تَبَّ ظَنَّ

صَبَّ مِمَّ اَيِّ شَرِّ صَلِّ مِتَّ قَلَّ رَبِّ

شَقًّا حُبًّا دَكًّا حَقُّ غَمِّ ضُرٍّ كُلُّ لُدًّا

صَفًّا غِلٍّ ظِلٍّ اُمٍّ جَمًّا حِلٌّ فَجٍّ عِزًّا

يَمُدُّ جَنَّةٍ كَرَّةً اُمَّةٍ يَفِرُّ يَحُضُّ

خَرُّوا سُجَّدًا بُكِيًّا هَيِّنٌ فَرِيًّا جِثِيًّا

هَمَّتْ تَبَّتْ حُقَّتْ مُتُّمْ خَفَّتْ تَخَلَّتْ

اُجِّلَتْ اُقِّتَتْ عُطِّلَتْ زُوِّجَتْ كَذَّبَتْ تَقَبَّلْ

STEP BY STEP

- Read the words that include a **Shaddah letter** without any hesitation.
  E.g. Rab-ba رَبَّ, Qal-la قَلَّ, An-na أَنَّ.

- Spell the words which include a **Shaddah letter**. E.g.

Step 1	Ra-Ba Fat-hah = Rab	رَبَّ
Step 2	Ba-Fat-hah = Ba	بَ
Step 3	Read the entire word, Rab-ba	رَبَّ

QUICK TIPS

Shaddah is actually two letters in one. Any time you see a Shaddah (ّ) you make a strong join. E.g. Alllaah, Muhammmad, Shadddah.

CHECKLIST

- I can read and spell the words that include a **Shaddah** fluently.
- I can read **each line fluently** (without hesitation or pausing).
- I can implement all the lessons learnt previously into this exercise.

Comments

EXERCISE 01 — DOUBLE SHADDAH WORDS

يُكَذِّبُ	صَبِيًّا	بَغِيًّا	جِبِلًّا	نُقَدِّسُ	تُحَدِّثُ
مُتَّقِينَ	مُصَلِّينَ	ٱلْأَوَّلِينَ	وَٱلنَّاسِ	وَدَّعَكَ	بِأَنَّهُمْ

يُبَيِّنُ	يَخْتَصُّ	أُنَاسِيَّ	مُصَدِّقًا	نُيَسِّرُهُ	يُبَدِّلُ
مُنْفَكِّينَ	إِنْسِيًّا	فِيهِنَّ	مَقْضِيًّا	مَرْضِيًّا	شَرْقِيًّا

يَتَوَفَّهُنَّ	ذُرِّيَّتَهُ	وَالزَّمَانَ	وَالنَّبِيِّينَ	أُمِّيُّونَ	
بِالسَّيِّئَةِ	لَيَبْطَأَنَّ	فَلَنَقُصَّنَّ	وَلَيُمَكِّنَنَّ	فَلَنُنَبِّئَنَّ	

يَشُقُّ	فَلْيُغَيِّرُنَّ	لَا تَتَّخِذَنَّ	لِلسَّيَّارَةِ	وَلَا السَّيِّئَةُ	
وَلَيَمَسَّنَّكُمْ	وَالصِّدِّيقِينَ	ٱلرَّبَّانِيُّونَ	لَأُمَنِّيَنَّهُمْ	يَضَّرَّعُونَ	

Completed on / /

STEP BY STEP

▸ Read and spell the words that include **two** Shaddah letters fluently.

Step 1	Ta Dhammah = Tu	تُ
Step 2	Ha-Daal Fat-hah = Had	حَدّ
Step 3	Join the two letters = Tu-Had	تُحَدّ
Step 4	Daal Kasrah = De	دِ
Step 5	Join all previous = Tu-Had-De	تُحَدِّ
Step 6	Tha Dhammah = Thu	ثُ
Step 7	Read the entire word = Tu-Had-De-Thu	تُحَدِّثُ

QUICK TIPS

Imagine the Shaddah letter is sticky, so whatever you join onto it sticks to it.
E.g. Alllaah, Muhammmad, Shadddah.

CHECKLIST

☑ I can read and spell the words that have two Shaddah's fluently

☑ I can read each line fluently (without hesitation or pausing).

☑ I can implement all the lessons learnt previously into this exercise.

EXERCISE 02 — DUAL WORDS

فَمَنْ اللهُ	اَضَلَّ اللهُ	فَضَّلَ اللهُ	وَكَلَّمَ اللهُ	اِلَّا الظَّنَّ
وَلِيِّ اللهُ	اَحَلَّ اللهُ	كُلَّ مُمَزَّقٍ	مَدَّ الظِّلَّ	اِلَّا الْحَقَّ
وَلِيُّكُمُ اللهُ	عَلَّمَكُمُ اللهُ	وَاتَّبَعَ مِلَّةَ	كُلَّمَا رُدُّوا	
وَيُحِقُّ الْحَقَّ	لَعَلَّهُمْ يَتَّقُونَ	ذُرِّيَّةً طَيِّبَةً	فَبَرَّأَهُ اللهُ	
وَاِنَّا لَنَظُنُّكَ	حُيِّيتُمْ بِتَحِيَّةٍ	ثُمَّ صَوَّرْنَكُمْ	وَاَشَدُّ قُوَّةً	
وَاُمُّهُ صِدِّيقَةٌ	اِنَّ الْعِزَّةَ لِلهِ	مُحِلِّي الصَّيْدِ	ثُمَّ لَاٰتِيَنَّهُمْ	
يَتَوَلَّى الصّٰلِحِينَ	اَكَّلُونَ لِلسُّحْتِ	اَلْاَنْفُسُ الشُّحَّ	يَقُصُّ الْحَقَّ	
وَقَدَّرَ فِي السَّرْدِ	فَاِنَّهَا مُحَرَّمَةٌ	بِالْبَيِّنٰتِ وَبِالزُّبُرِ	سُنَّتَ الْاَوَّلِينَ	

- ▸ Read the dual and plural words that include a Shaddah in each word.
- ▸ Spell the dual and plural words that include a Shaddah in each word.

Step 1	Alif-Laam Kasrah = Il	إلّ
Step 2	Laam-Dhaa Fat-hah = Ladh	لَّا الظّ
Step 3	Join the two letters = Il-Ladh	إلَّا الظّ
Step 4	Dhaa-Noon Fat-hah = Dhan	ظَّنَ
Step 5	Join all previous = Il-Ladh-Dhan	إلَّا الظَّنَ
Step 6	Noon Fat-hah = Na	نَ
Step 7	Join all previous = Il-Ladh-Dhan-Na	إلَّا الظَّنَّ

QUICK TIPS

- ▸ Two words with two sticky letters.
- ▸ Before reading it, point out the Shaddahs, so when you read it you can apply the Shaddahs at the right place.

CHECKLIST

- ✓ I can read and spell the dual words that have Shaddah fluently.
- ✓ I can read each line fluently (without hesitation or pausing).
- ✓ I can implement all the lessons learnt previously into this exercise.

EXERCISE 03 — DUAL WORDS

اِلَّا الَّذِينَ	مِنَ الطَّيِّبٰتِ	فَاَصْلَحْتُ	اِنَّ الَّذِينَ
فَلَمَّا تَغَشّٰىهَا	رَبُّ الشِّعْرٰى	فَلَهُنَّ الثُّمُنُ	اِنَّ السَّاعَةَ
بِالَّيْلِ وَالنَّهَارِ	وَقَرَّبْنٰهُ نَجِيًّا	وَيُوَلُّونَ الدُّبُرَ	فَلِاُمِّهِ الثُّلُثُ
وَسَخَّرَ الشَّمْسَ	وَاِذَا مَسَّهُ الشَّرُّ	عَلَّمَكُمُ السِّحْرَ	ذُرِّيَّتِهِمَا النُّبُوَّةَ
فَاتَّخِذُوهُ عَدُوًّا	اَنِّي مَسَّنِيَ الضُّرُّ		اَلطَّيِّبٰتُ لِلطَّيِّبِينَ
اِذْ يُغَشِّيكُمُ النُّعَاسَ	لَا تُكَلَّفُ اِلَّا نَفْسَكَ	يُنْسِيَنَّكَ الشَّيْطَانُ
وَمَا عَلَّمْنٰهُ الشِّعْرَ	لَا تَتَّبِعْتُمُ الشَّيْطَانَ	يَتَّبِعُونَ الشَّهَوٰتِ
يُحِبُّهُمْ وَيُحِبُّونَهُ	وَالسَّارِقُ وَالسَّارِقَةُ	اَوْ لَتَعُودُنَّ فِي مِلَّتِنَا

STEP BY STEP

↠ Read and spell the dual and plural words that include Shaddah letters in them fluently.

Step 1	Alif-Laam Kasrah = Il	اِلّ
Step 2	Laam-Laam Fat-hah = Lal	لَّالَ
Step 3	Join the two letters = Il-Lal	اِلَّالَ
Step 4	La Fat-hah = La	لَ
Step 5	Join all previous = Il-Lal-La	اِلَّالَّ
Step 6	Thaal Ya Kasrah = Thee	ذِيْ
Step 7	Join all previous = Il-Lal-La-Thee	اِلَّالَّذِيْ
Step 8	Noon Fat-hah = Na	نَ
Step 9	Read the entire word = Il-Lal-La-Thee-Na	اِلَّالَّذِيْنَ

QUICK TIPS

↠ **Do not stretch** Fat-hah, Kasrah and Dhammah letters.
Split the long words into smaller chunks, practice them and then read them together.

CHECKLIST

☑ I can **read and spell** the dual and plural words that have Shaddah in them fluently.

☑ I can read each line fluently (without hesitation or pausing).

☑ I can implement all the lessons learnt previously into this exercise.

Comments

GRADE 10

The Prophet ﷺ said:
"The best amongst you is he who learns the Qur'aan and teaches it to others."
(Muslim)

OVERVIEW

LESSON 19 > SILENT LETTERS IN WORDS

If a letter appears in a word without a Harakah, it will not be pronounced or even spelt. These are called **'Silent Letters'** which are generally **'Alif', 'Waw' and 'Ya'**.
They have been highlighted in red on the first two lines.
- ▶ Silent Alif is normally written between two words.
- ▶ Silent Waw is normally written in the middle of the word.
- ▶ Silent Ya is normally written at the end of the word.

LESSON 20 > SILENT ALIF

Whenever an Alif comes with a **small circle above it**, it will be ignored. There are only 17 words in the Qur'aan that include this silent Alif, they have all been mentioned in this lesson.

LESSON 21 > SPECIAL WORDS

There are only 4 words in the Qur'aan that have both the **'Seen'** and **'Saad'** together.
Whenever the letter Ta comes after the Seen or Saad, then Seen will be read.
- ▶ The letters that are to be read are in green and the ones that are not supposed to be read are in red.
- ▶ There is one word in the Qur'aan that has a Madd Kasrah beneath it, but is pronounced in a **different manner**.

LESSON 22 > WORDS WITH A JERKING SOUND

If a Hamzah with a Sukoon appears on an **Alif, Waw or Ya**, the letters Alif, Waw and Ya, **will be ignored** and the Hamzah will be read with a slight jerking sound.
When a Sukoon appears on an Alif, the Alif will be referred to as a Hamzah and will be read with a **slight jerk**.
The student should always read each line without hesitation or pausing to help build consistency and speed.

LESSON 19 — SILENT LETTERS IN WORDS

كَفٰى	اٰبٰى	اٰتٰى	اِلٰى	عَلٰى	
ضُحٰى	اَبْقٰى	اٰوٰى	سُدًى	هَوٰى	
اَخْفٰى	يَحْيٰى	طَغٰى	سُوٰى	هَدٰى	
تَنْسٰى	فَاَوْحٰى	صَلٰوةً	اُخْرٰى	تَرْقٰى	
لِتَشْقٰى	فَتُلْقٰى	كُسْلٰى	تَرْضٰى	زَكٰوةً	

يَشْوِى الْوُجُوْهَ	عَلَى الْاِنْسَانِ	زَهَقَ الْبَاطِلُ	قُرْاٰنَ الْفَجْرِ
ذِى الْقَرْنَيْنِ	هُنَالِكَ الْوَلَايَةُ	وَزِدْنٰهُمْ هُدًى	يٰمُوْسٰى مَسْحُوْرًا
عَلَى الْعَرْشِ اسْتَوٰى	مَا اسْتَطَاعُوْا لَهٗ	يَوْمَ الْقِيٰمَةِ اَعْلٰى	فَتَرَى الْمُجْرِمِيْنَ

STEP BY STEP

• Read the words that include a silent letter.
E.g. 'Alaa عَلَى, Elaa إِلَى, Ataa أَتَى.

• Spell the words which include a **silent letter**. E.g.

Step 1	'Ayn, Fat-hah = 'A	عَ
Step 2	Laam, Madd Fat-ha = Laa	لَى
Step 3	Read the the entire word = 'A-laa	عَلَى

QUICK TIPS

When you see an Alif ا, Waw و or Ya ى without any harakah and the letter after has a Sukoon or a Shaddah, you will not read or spell them.

CHECKLIST

- ☉ I can **read and spell** the **single and double words** that include silent letters.
- ☉ I can read each line **fluently in one breath** (without hesitation or pausing).
- ☉ I can implement all the lessons learnt previously into this exercise.

LESSON 20: SILENT ALIF

أَنَا

| أَنَا نَذِيرٌ | أَنَا عَابِدٌ | أَنَا أَخُوكَ | نَدْعُوا |

| ثَمُودَا | لِيَرْبُوا | لَكِنَّا هُوَ | لِتَتْلُوا |

| لِيَبْلُوا | وَمَلَأَيْهِ | أَفَائِنْ | سَلْسِلَا |
| قَوَارِيرَا | وَلَا أَوْضَعُوا | لَا إِلَى الْجَحِيمِ | وَنَبْلُوا أَخْبَارَكُمْ |

STEP BY STEP

• Read the words that include a silent Alif. E.g. Ana أَنَا , Ana-natheeroon أَنَاْنَذِيْرٌ , Ana-'Aabi-doon أَنَاْعَابِدٌ .

• Spell the words which include a **silent Alif** fluently. E.g.

Step 1	Alif Fat-hah = A	اَ
Step 2	Noon Fat-hah = Na	نَ
Step 3	Read the entire word, A-na	اَنَا

When a small circle comes on an Alif اَنَاْ it cancels it.

QUICK TIPS

CHECKLIST

✓ I can **read and spell** the words that include the silent Alif.

✓ I can read each line fluently in one breath (without hesitation or pausing).

✓ I can implement all the lessons learnt previously into this exercise.

LESSON 21

SPECIAL WORDS

Surah Al A'raaf.

Surah Al Baqarah.

Surah Al Ghaashiyah.

Surah At Toor.

Identify which letters to read in these four words that include "Seen" and "Saad".

Pronounce the sound of the Madd Kasrah "Maj-ray-haa". The letter "Ra" will be pronounced like the word "Rare" in English.

STEP BY STEP

◆▶ Read the words that include a Seen and Saad.
E.g. Wa-yab-sutu وَيَبْسُطْ , Basta-tan بَصْطَةً ,
Humul-musaytiroona هُمُ الْمُصَيْطِرُونَ ,
Bi-musaytirin بِمُصَيْطِرٍ .

◆▶ Spell the words that include a Seen and Saad. E.g.

Step 1	Waw, Fat-hah = Wa	وَ
Step 2	Ya, Ba, Fat-hah = Yab	يَبْ
Step 3	Join the two words, Wa-Yab	وَيَبْ
Step 4	Seen, Dhammah = Su	سُ
Step 5	Join all previous, Wa-Yab-Su	وَيَبْسُ
Step 6	Ta, Dhammah = Tu	طُ
Step 7	Read the entire word, Wa-Yab-Su-Tu	وَيَبْسُطْ

If after the letters Seen & Saad the letter Ta ط comes, the letter Seen س will be read not Saad. E.g. وَيَبْسُطْ

CHECKLIST

✓ I can **read and spell** the words which have the letters **Seen and Saad**.

✓ I can read each line **fluently in one breath** (without hesitation or pausing).

✓ I can implement all the lessons learnt previously into this exercise.

LESSON 22: WORDS WITH A JERKING SOUND

يَأْبَ   بَأْسٍ   نَأْتِ   كَأْسًا   شَأْنٌ

وَأْمُرْ   وَرِئْيًا   وَلُؤُا   يُؤْمِنُ   قَرَأْتَ

يُؤْتِينِ   جِئْتُكُمْ   اَخْطَأْتُمْ   يُؤْفَكُ   يُؤْذَنَ

مَأْوَاهُمْ   تُؤْثِرُونَ   مُؤْصَدَةٌ   فَيُؤْخَذُ   آيَأْمُرُكُمْ

وَهُوَمُؤْمِنٌ   بَلْ تُؤْثِرُونَ   مَايُؤْمَرُونَ   لَايَسْتَأْخِرُونَ

يَأْكُلُ مِنْهَا   أَبْلِغْهُ مَأْمَنَهُ   وَكَأْسًا دِهَاقًا   تَأْكُلُوا جَمِيعًا

فَأْتِيَا فِرْعَوْنَ   وَلِلْأَرْضِ ائْتِيَا   يَأْتِينِي بِعَرْشِهَا   لَقَدْ جِئْتِ شَيْئًا

يُؤْتِيهِمْ أُجُورَهُمْ   يَأْجُوجَ وَمَأْجُوجَ   وَأْتُونِ مُسْلِمِينَ   يَأْلَمُونَ كَمَاتَأْلَمُونَ

- ▸ Read the words that have Hamzah with a Sukoon above them fluently.
  E.g. Ya'ba يَأْبَ, Ba'sin بَأْسٍ, Na'te نَأْتِ.

- ▸ Spell the words that include a Hamzah with a Sukoon E.g.

Step 1	Ya, Hamzah, Fat-hah = Ya'	يَأْ
Step 2	Ba, Fat-hah = Ba	بَ
Step 3	Read the entire word, Ya'-ba	يَأْبَ

QUICK TIPS

If Hamzah comes with a Sukoon on an Alif, Waw or Ya. The Alif, Waw or Ya will become silent and will be read with a slight jerking sound يَأْبَ .

Sometimes Alif will come with a Sukoon on it but without a Hamzah. Cancel the Alif and read with a jerking sound بَأْسٍ .

- ✓ I can read and spell the words with a jerking sound which have a **Sukoon above a Hamzah** and a **Sukoon above a silent Alif** fluently.
- ✓ I can read each line **fluently in one breath** (without hesitation or pausing).
- ✓ I can implement all the lessons learnt previously into this exercise.

GRADE 11

The Prophet ﷺ said:

"The one who was devoted to the Qur'aan will be told on the Day of Resurrection: "Recite and ascend (in ranks) as you used to recite when you were in the world. Your rank will be at the last Ayah you recite."

(Abu Dawud and Tirmidhi)

OVERVIEW

Small Madd is to stretch for around 2 seconds

- The small Madd ⌒ indicates that the letter will be stretched for around two seconds.
- A small Madd is always in need of a Harakah before it. It can never come by itself rather it stretches the sound of the Harakah before it.
  E.g. If a Fat-hah comes before a small madd, the sound of the Fat-hah will be stretched.
- Ensure the student is confident in spelling this lesson.

Big Madd is to stretch for around 4 seconds

- The Big Madd ⌒ indicates the letter will be stretched for around 3 to 4 seconds.
- A Big Madd is always in need of a Harakah before it. It can never come by itself rather it stretches the sound of the Harakah before it.
  E.g. If a Fat-hah comes before a Big madd, the sound of the Fat-hah will be stretched.
- Ensure the student is confident in spelling this lesson.

Long stretch followed by a strong join

- If after a Big Madd a Shaddah appears, then you must stretch and do a strong join for around 3 to 4 seconds: جَآٰ
- Ensure the student is confident in spelling this lesson.

LESSON 23: SMALL MADD

اِلَّآ اِذَا	حَتَّىٰٓ اِذَا	اِنَّمَآ اَنَا	اِلٰٓى اُمِّهٖ
وَلَآ اَقُوۡلُ	بِمَآ اَنۡزَلَ	اَبَآ اَحَدٍ	اِنَّآ اٰمَنَّا
فَلَهٗٓ اَسۡلَمُوۡا	لَمَّآ اٰتَيۡتُكُمۡ	اِلٰٓى اَنۡفُسِهِمۡ	لَهٗٓ اَصۡحٰبُ
يٰٓاِبۡرٰهِيۡمُ	لَهٗٓ اَهۡلَهٗ	فَاِذَآ اُوۡذِىَ	اِنِّىۡٓ اَحۡبَبۡتُ

فَلَآ اُقۡسِمُ بِالشَّفَقِ	اِنَّ اِلَيۡنَآ اِيَابَهُمۡ
فَيَقُوۡلُ رَبِّىۡٓ اَكۡرَمَنِ	لَا يَصۡلٰىهَآ اِلَّا الۡاَشۡقَى
لَآ اَعۡبُدُ مَا تَعۡبُدُوۡنَ	اَلَّذِىۡٓ اَنۡقَضَ ظَهۡرَكَ
وَمَآ اَدۡرٰىكَ مَا سِجِّيۡنٌ	وَالَّذِىۡٓ اَخۡرَجَ الۡمَرۡعٰى

STEP BY STEP

• ▶ Read the words that include a small Madd fluently. E.g. Il-laaa-Ithaa اِلَّاۤ اِذَا , Hat-Taaa-Ithaa حَتّٰۤ اِذَا , In-namaaa-ana اِنَّمَاۤ اَنَا .

• ▶ Spell the words which include a small Madd E.g.

Step 1	Alif, Laam Kasrah = Il	اِلْ
Step 2	Laam, Alif Fat-hah, Madd = Laaa	لَاۤ
Step 3	Join the two, Il-Laaa	اِلَّاۤ
Step 4	Alif, Kasrah = E	اِ
Step 5	Join all previous, Il-Laaa-E	اِلَّاۤ اِ
Step 6	Thaal, Alif, Fat-hah = Thaa	ذَا
Step 7	Read the entire word, Il-Laaa-E-Thaa	اِلَّاۤ اِذَا

• ▶ Stretch the small Madd for 2 seconds.

• ▶ When a Madd comes with a letter that is already being stretched then the sound of the letter will be stretched for 2 seconds in total.

☑ I can **read and spell** the words that include a **small Madd** fluently.

☑ I can read **each line fluently** (without hesitation or pausing).

☑ I can implement all the lessons learnt previously into this exercise.

LESSON 24 — BIG MADD

بِلِقَآءٍ	يَشَآءُ	دُعَآءٍ	اٰبَآءٍ
وَضِيَآءً	اِيْتَآءِ	تَبُوْٓاَ	يُضِىْٓءُ
شُهَدَآءَ	هَنِيْٓئًا	شَعَآئِرَ	سَيْنَآءَ
لِلطَّآئِفِيْنَ	اَدْعِيَآئِهِمْ	وَاَحِبَّاؤُهٗ	قَآئِلُهَا

لَآ اَتَّبِعُ اَهْوَآءَكُمْ	اَسَآءُوا السُّوْٓاٰى
يَوْمَ نَطْوِى السَّمَآءَ	اَلَا سَآءَ مَا يَحْكُمُوْنَ
يَوْمَ تُبْلَى السَّرَآئِرُ	اَلْآنَ اِنَّ اَوْلِيَآءَ اللّٰهِ
بَوَّأْنَا بَنِىْٓ اِسْرَآئِيْلَ	اٰبَآءَنَا الضَّرَّآءُ وَالسَّرَّآءُ

STEP BY STEP

- Read the words that include a **big Madd** fluently. E.g. Aa-baaa-e اِبَاءِ , Du-'Aaaa-e دُعَاءِ , Ya-shaaa-o يَشَاءُ .

- Spell the words which include a **big Madd** E.g.

Step 1	Alif, Madd Fat-hah = Aa	اَ
Step 2	Ba, Alif, Fat-hah, Madd = Baaa	بَا
Step 3	Join the two, Aa-Baaa	اَبَا
Step 4	Hamzah, Kasrah = E	ءِ
Step 5	Read the entire word, Aa-Baaa-E	اِبَاءِ

QUICK TIPS

Stretch the big Madd for 3 to 4 seconds. (Same as small Madd but longer stretch).

CHECKLIST

- I can **read and spell** the dual words that have a **small** and **big** Madd fluently.
- I can read **each line fluently** (without hesitation or pausing).
- I can implement all the lessons learnt previously into this exercise.

Comments

LESSON 25: BIG MADD FOLLOWED BY A SHADDAH

جَآنٌّ	ضَآلًّا	آللّٰهُ	كَآفَّةً
دَآبَّةٍ	آمِّينَ	خَآصَّةً	شَآقُّوا
بِرَآدِّي	حَآجَّكَ	تَتَّبِعَآنِّ	ظَآنِّينَ
ضَآلِّينَ	تَحُضُّونَ	ءَآلذَّكَرَيْنِ	أَتُحَآجُّوٓنِّي

اِنَّا رَآدُّوهُ اِلَيْكِ	لَرَآدُّكَ اِلٰى مَعَادٍ
اِنَّ هٰٓؤُلَآءِ لَضَآلُّونَ	فَاِذَا جَآءَتِ الصَّآخَّةُ
اَلْحَآقَّةُ مَا الْحَآقَّةُ	يُوَآدُّونَ مَنْ حَآدَّ اللّٰهَ
اِنْسٌ قَبْلَهُمْ وَلَا جَآنٌّ	اِنَّ الَّذِينَ يُحَآدُّونَ اللّٰهَ

•▶ Read the words that include a big **Madd** followed by a **Shaddah** letter fluently. E.g. Jaaan-nun جَآنّ , Dhaaal-lan ضَآلّ , Aaaal-laahu آللَّٰه .

•▶ Spell the words which include a **big Madd** followed by a **Shaddah** letter E.g.

Step 1	Jeem, Noon, Fat-hah, Madd = Jaaann	جَآن
Step 2	Noon, Dhamma-tayn = Nun	نٌ
Step 3	Read the entire word, Jaaann-Nun	جَآنّ

•▶ Stretch the sound for around 3 to 4 seconds and join straight onto the Shaddah letter.

•▶ Ensure a strong join is done instantly after a long stretch.

☑ I can **read and spell** the words that include a big **Madd followed by a Shaddah** letter fluently.

☑ I can read **each line fluently** (without any hesitation or pausing).

☑ I can implement all the lessons learnt previously into this exercise.

GRADE 12

The Prophet ﷺ said:

"Whoever recites a letter from the Book of Allaah, he will be credited with a good deed, and a good deed gets a ten-fold reward. I do not say that Alif-Laam-Meem is one letter, but Alif is a letter, Laam is a letter and Meem is a letter."

(Muslim)

OVERVIEW

LESSON 26 › QALQALAH

Qalqalah is to pronounce a letter with a slight bounce

- When any of the letters of Qalqalah  appear with a Sukoon, the letter will be read with a slight bounce.
- The same rule will apply if any of these letters come with a Shaddah on them at the end of the word only.

LESSON 27 › GHUNNAH

Ghunnah means to stretch with a deep nasal sound

- When a Noon  or Meem appears with a Shaddah, the sound will be stretched in the nose for a second or so.

LESSON 28 › IZHAAR

Izhaar is to read the Noon saakin or Tanween clearly without any nasal stretching sound

- To read the sound of the Noon saakin or Tanween clearly (without Ghunnah).
- If after a Noon Saakin or Tanween any of these 6 throat letters appear  there will be Izhaar, i.e. no Ghunnah.

Note: Tanween = Fat-ha-tayn, Kasra-tayn and Dhamma-tayn  .

LESSON 26: QALQALAH

ق ط ب ج د

وَعَدْلًا	أَقْلَامٌ	أَطْهَرُ	عِجْلًا	عَبْدًا
اَعْتَدْنَا	بِقِطْعٍ	يَطْبَعُ	نَجْعَل	اِذْهَب
فَاخْرُجْ	أُقْسِمُ	فَاهْبِطْ	تَجْهَرُ	اَبْصَرَ
صَدْرِي	اَقْلِعِي	بِعِجْلٍ	خَطْبُكَ	يَبْسُطُ
مَقْطُوعٌ	تَجْعَل	صَدْرُكَ	يَنْبُؤُ	تُسْقِطْ
تَبْتَئِسْ	يَلْتَقِطْهُ	تَدْمِيرًا	لَتُبْدِي	فَاجْتَبٰهُ
تُعَذِّبْهُمْ	وَاجْتَبَيْنَا	تَبْسُطُهَا	أَوِاطْرَحُوهُ	اَخْرَجْتَهَا
تُطْعِمُونَ	رَزَقْنٰكُمْ	حَسِبْتُمْ	مُجْرِمُونَ	خَلَقْنٰكُمْ

    Completed on D D / M M / YEAR

STEP BY STEP

•▶ Read the words which include a Qalqalah fluently

•▶ Spell the words which include a Qalqalah (refer to Lesson 06: Sukoon).

•▶ Identify the Qalqalah letters confidently

Qalqalah is to read a letter with a slight bounce

QUICK TIPS

•▶ Make sure the bounce of the Qalqalah is only a third of a Fat-hah sound.

•▶ Remember this one word *Qutubujad*, it has all the letters of Qalqalah ق ط ب ج د, which should help you remember them.
Qu-tu-bu-jad = قُطْبُجَدْ

CHECKLIST

☑ I can **read and spell** the words that include a **Qalqalah** properly.

☑ I can read **each line fluently** (without hesitation or pausing).

☑ I can implement all the lessons learnt previously into this exercise.

LESSON 27 — GHUNNAH

كُنَّا	تَبَّتْ	عَنَّا	مِمَّا	جَنَّ
صُمٌّ	وَجَنَّتٍ	وَلَمَّا	اٰمَنَّا	هَمَّ
لَتَعُودُنَّ	أُمَّةٌ	جَهَنَّمَ	عَمَّا	فِيهِنَّ
اَيَّةً	فَلَنَسْئَلَنَّ	وَأُمِّي	لَيَمَسَّنَّ	غُمَّةً
لَنَكُونَنَّ	وَهَمُّوا	وَالنَّبِيّنَ	ذِمَّةً	لَنَظُنُّكَ
لَاَمْلَئَنَّ	الْاَمِّينَ	لَاٰتِيَنَّهُمْ	اَهَمَّتْهُمْ	مَكَّنَّكُمْ
لَيُؤْمِنَنَّ	فَعُمِّيَتْ	لَيَزِيدَنَّ	فَاْتُوا	فَلَنَقُصَّنَّ
يُنْسِيَنَّكَ	سَمَّعُونَ	فَتَيَمَّمُوا	مُتَعَمِّدًا	لَايَفْتِنَنَّكُمْ

• Read the words that include a Ghunnah

• Spell the words which include a Ghunnah (refer to Lesson 10: Shaddah).

• Identify the Ghunnah letters confidently.

Ghunnah is to stretch with a strong nasal sound

Do a Ghunnah when you see the letters ﻥّ and ﻡّ.

QUICK TIPS

CHECKLIST

✓ I can **read and spell** the words that **include a Ghunnah** properly.

✓ I can read **each line fluently** (without hesitation or pausing).

✓ I can implement all the lessons learnt previously into this exercise.

LESSON 28 — IZHAAR

مِنْ هَادٍ	مَنْ عَمِلَ	مِنْ حَرَجٍ	مِنْ خَوْفٍ
مَنْ أَعْطَى	وَمِنْ خِزْيِ	يَوْمٍ عَسِرٍ	عَذَابًا أَلِيمًا
مَثَلًا عَبْدًا	لِيَوْمٍ عَظِيمٍ	حُورٌ عِينٌ	حَكِيمٌ خَبِيرٌ
وَإِنْ عَاقَبْتُمْ	نَارٌ حَامِيَةٌ	لَا خَوْفٌ عَلَيْهِمْ	وَلِمَنْ خَافَ
كَلِمَةٍ خَبِيثَةٍ	أُمَّةٍ أَجَلٌ	شَفَاعَةً حَسَنَةً	قُرْآنًا عَجَبًا
كَذَّابٌ أَشِرٌ	مِنْ أَقْطَارِهَا	بَيَاتًا أَوْ نَهَارًا	طَيْرًا أَبَابِيلَ
مِنْ عَيْنٍ آنِيَةٍ	أَشِحَّةً عَلَيْكُمْ	فِي يَوْمٍ عَاصِفٍ	وَلَا تَحْزَنْ عَلَيْهِمْ
خَيْرَاتٌ حِسَانٌ	وَعَبْقَرِيٍّ حِسَانٍ	بِسَلَامٍ آمِنِينَ	مُخْتَلِفًا أَلْوَانُهُ

STEP BY STEP

•▶ Read the words that include a **Izhaar**

 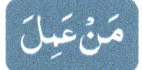 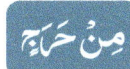 مِنْ هَادٍ

•▶ Spell the words that include a **Izhaar** (refer to Lesson 06: Sukoon)

•▶ Identify the **Throat letters** confidently

Izhaar is to read the Noon saakin or Tanween clearly without any nasal stretching sound.

QUICK TIPS

Izhaar is to read the Noon Saakin نْ and Tanween clearly ٍ ٌ ً , i.e. without Ghunnah.

CHECKLIST

☑ I can **read and spell** the words that **include Izhaar** properly.

☑ I can read each line **fluently in one breath** (without hesitation or pausing).

☑ I can implement all the lessons learnt previously into this exercise.

GRADE 13

The Prophet ﷺ said:

"Any group of people that assemble in one of the Houses of Allaah to recite the Book of Allaah, learning and teaching it, tranquility will descend upon them, mercy will engulf them, angels will surround them and Allaah will make mention of them to those (the angels) in His proximity."

(Muslim)

OVERVIEW

LESSON 29 > **RULE OF THE LETTER RA**

Full mouth with 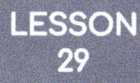 and

- Ra with a Fat-hah رَ or Dhammah رُ will be read with a full mouth sound (the same rule applies if the Ra has a Shaddah on it).
- Ra with a Kasrah رِ will be read with an empty mouth sound.
- If Ra has a Sukoon on it and a Fat-hah تَرْ or Dhammah يُرْ is joining onto it, then the letter Ra will be read with a full mouth sound.
- However, if a Kasrah is joining onto it شِرْ , then the letter Ra will be read with an empty mouth.
- The green colour indicates the full mouth Ra and the red colour indicates the empty mouth Ra.

LESSON 30 > **RULE OF THE WORD ALLAAH**

Full mouth with 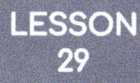 and

- If a Fat-hah or Dhammah is joining onto the word Allaah then the letter Laam in the word Allaah will be pronounced with a full mouth sound:
- If a Kasrah is joining onto the word Allaah, then the letter Laam in the word Allaah will be pronounced with an empty mouth sound: يَرْفَعِاللهِ
- The green colour indicates the full mouth Laam and the red colour indicates the empty mouth Laam.

LESSON 29: RULE OF THE LETTER 'RA'

فِيهِ الرَّحْمَةُ	فَالْمُورِيٰتِ قَدْحًا	تَرْهَقُهَا قَتَرَةٌ
لِسَعْيِهَا رَاضِيَةٌ	يُرْسِلُ الرِّيٰحَ	مَرْفُوعَةٍ مُّطَهَّرَةٍ
مِنْ ضَرِيعٍ	خَلَقَهُ فَقَدَّرَهُ	فَأَكْرَمَهُ وَنَعَّمَهُ
فِي صُحُفٍ مُّكَرَّمَةٍ	وَاِلٰى رَبِّكَ فَارْغَبْ	رُءُوسَكُمْ وَمُقَصِّرِينَ
رِيحًا صَرْصَرًا	عُرُبًا أَتْرَابًا	فَرَوْحٌ وَّرَيْحَانٌ
فَالزَّاجِرٰتِ زَجْرًا	كُلُّ أَمْرٍ مُّسْتَقِرٌّ	فِيهَا سُرُرٌ مَّرْفُوعَةٌ
هٰذَا عَارِضٌ مُّمْطِرُنَا	اِنَّ مَعَ الْعُسْرِ يُسْرًا	كُلَّ شِرْبٍ مُّحْتَضَرٌ
فَشَارِبُونَ شُرْبَ الْهِيمِ	فَقَدَّرَ عَلَيْهِ رِزْقَهُ	أُولٰئِكَ هُمْ خَيْرُ الْبَرِيَّةِ

STEP BY STEP

• Read the letter **Ra** as a **full mouth letter** when it has a **Fat-hah or Dhammah** above it

• Read the letter **Ra** as an **empty mouth letter** when it has a **Kasrah** beneath it

The letter Ra will be read with a full mouth when it comes with a 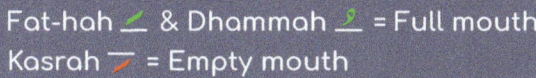 or .

Fat-hah & Dhammah = Full mouth
Kasrah = Empty mouth

QUICK TIPS

CHECKLIST

- I can read the letter **Ra** as a **full mouth letter**.
- I can read **each line fluently** (without hesitation or pausing).
- I can implement all the lessons learnt previously into this exercise.

 **LESSON 30 — RULE OF THE WORD ALLAAH**

حِزْبُ اللهِ	يَرْفَعِ اللهُ	كَتَبَ اللهُ	حُرِّمَتِ اللهِ
وَعَدَ اللهُ	يُشَاقِّ اللهَ	أَمْرَ اللهِ	لِذِكْرِ اللهِ
هُوَ اللهُ	وَجْهَ اللهِ	عَفَا اللهُ	غَضِبَ اللهُ
فِي سَبِيلِ اللهِ	فَاتَّقُوا اللهَ	أَطِيعُوا اللهَ	يَهْدِي اللهُ
فَيَنْسَخُ اللهُ	أَنْ هَدَانَا اللهُ	اُعْبُدُوا اللهَ	يَبْعَثُهُمُ اللهُ
شَعَائِرَ اللهِ	مِنْ دُونِ اللهِ	عَنْ ذِكْرِ اللهِ	أَنِ اشْكُرْ لِلهِ
قُلْ صَدَقَ اللهُ	اِتَّقُوا اللهَ حَقَّ تُقَاتِهِ		أَعْدَاءِ اللهِ النَّارُ
وَمَا مِنْ إِلٰهٍ إِلَّا اللهُ	يَضْرِبُ اللهُ الْأَمْثَالَ	لَمْ تَكْفُرُونَ بِآيَاتِ اللهِ	

STEP BY STEP

•▸ Read the word **Allaah** with a **full mouth** when it has a **Fat-hah** or **Dhammah** before it

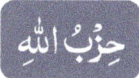 

•▸ Read the word **Allaah** with an **empty mouth** when it has a **Kasrah** before it

The word اللهُ will be read with a full mouth when a ◡ or ◡ is joining onto it.

QUICK TIPS

Fat-hah ◡ & Dhammah ◡ = Full mouth
Kasrah ◡ = Empty mouth

CHECKLIST

☑ I can read the word **Allaah** with a full mouth.

☑ I can read **each line fluently** (without hesitation or pausing).

☑ I can implement all the lessons learnt previously into this exercise.

GRADE 14

The Prophet ﷺ said:

"Read the Qur'aan, for it will come as an intercessor for its reciters on the Day of Resurrection."

(Muslim)

OVERVIEW

LESSON 31 > **IDGHAAM AND SILENT LETTERS**

To merge two letters together

- Whenever a **Saakin letter** ࣲ and **Shaddah letter** ࣲ come together, the Saakin letter will become silent and will not be read or spelt. E.g. The **Kaaf** will join straight onto the **Ta**: كِدْتَّ

LESSON 32 > **IDGHAAM**

Idghaam - Merge two letters together

- There are 6 letters of Idghaam ي ر م ل و ن
- There are 2 types of Idghaam:
  1. Idghaam without Ghunnah
  2. Idghaam with Ghunnah

Idghaam without Ghunnah

- If after a **Noon Saakin** or **Tanween** any of these 2 letters ر & ل appear there will be **Idghaam without Ghunnah**.
- Idghaam without Ghunnah means to join directly without any sound in the nose. E.g. The **Fa** joins onto the **Laam** without any sound coming from the nose: اُفٍّ لَّكُمْ

Idghaam with Ghunnah

- If after a **Noon Saakin** or **Tanween** any of these 4 letters ي ن م و (Yanmoo) appear there will be **Idghaam with Ghunnah**.
- Idghaam with Ghunnah means to stretch the sound of these letters in the nose when joining. E.g. The **Laam** joins onto the **Ya** but with the sound coming from the nose: رَجُلٌ يُّرِيْدُ

LESSON 31: IDGHAAM AND SILENT LETTERS

| كِدتَّ | اَحَطتُّ | قُل لَّوْ | عَبَدتُّمْ | بَل رَّفَعَ |

| اَقُل لَّكَ | بَسَطتَّ | اَن رَّبَطْنَا | وَقَد دَّخَلُوا | اَن عَبَدتَّ |

| وُلِدتُّ | قُل رَّبِّ | لَاَرَدتُّ | وَجَدتُّمْ | وَعَدتَّهُمْ |

| يُدْرِكْكُمْ | قَد تَّبَيَّنَ | حَصَدتُّمْ | فَرَّطتُّمْ | وَاذْكُرْ رَّبَّكَ |

| اَلَمْ نَخْلُقْكُّمْ | وَاِنْ اَرَدتُّمْ | بَل لَّا تُكْرِمُونَ | اِضْرِب بِّعَصَاكَ |

| اَوَاوَنَصَرُوا | رَبِحَت تِّجَارَتُهُمْ | وَقَالَت طَّآئِفَةٌ | وَارْكَب مَّعَنَا |

STEP BY STEP

→ Read the words which include a **Saakin** and **Shaddah** letter without spelling. E.g. كَنَتْ اَحْطَتْ قُلْ لُو

→ Spell the words which include a **Saakin** and **Shaddah** letter. E.g.

Step 1	Kaaf, Ta, Kasrah = Kit	كِتْ
Step 2	Ta, Fat-hah = Ta	تَ
Step 3	Read the entire word, Kit-Ta	كِتَ

Merge two letters together by cancelling the Saakin letter and joining straight onto the Shaddah letter.

Remember, if a letter with a Sukoon comes before a letter with a Shaddah, it will be cancelled.

QUICK TIPS

CHECKLIST

✓ I can **read and spell** the words that include a **silent letter**.

✓ I can read **each line fluently** (without hesitation or pausing).

✓ I can implement all the lessons learnt previously into this exercise.

LESSON 32: IDGHAAM WITHOUT GHUNNAH

أُفٍّ لَّكُمْ	نُوحٌ رَّبِّ	جَنَّتٍ لَّهُمْ	زَبَدًا رَّابِيًا
مِنْ لَّدُنْهُ	مَنْ رَّحِمَ	لَئِنْ لَّمْ	مِنْ رَّبِّكَ
أَنْ رَّآهُ	عِيدًا لِّأَوَّلِنَا	جَمِيعٌ لَّدَيْنَا	أَخْذَةً رَّابِيَةً
أَشْتَاتًا لِّيُرَوْا	مِنْ رُّسُلِهِ	أَنْ لَّمْ يَرَهُ	عِيشَةٍ رَّاضِيَةٍ
ثَمَرَةٍ رِّزْقًا	مَتَاعًا لَّكُمْ	مِنْ رَّأْسِهِ	بَقَرَةٌ لَّا فَارِضٌ
غَفُورٌ رَّحِيمٌ	لَمْ يَكُنْ لَّهُ	تَوَّابٌ رَّحِيمٌ	حَقٌّ لِّلسَّائِلِ
زَبَدًا رَّابِيًا	هُدًى لِّلْمُتَّقِينَ	خَيْرٌ لِّأَنْفُسِهِمْ	شِهَابًا رَّصَدًا
أَنْ رَّا بُرْهَانَ	خَافِضَةٌ رَّافِعَةٌ	كَأَنْ لَّمْ يَغْنَوْا	مِنْ رِّزْقِ اللهِ

STEP BY STEP

• Read the words that include **Idghaam**.
  E.g. جَنَّتٌ أَلْهَمَّ   نُوحٌ رَبِّ   أَنْ لَكُمْ

• Spell the words which include a **Idghaam**

Step 1	Alif, Fa, Dhammah = Uf	أُفْ
Step 2	Fa, Laam, Kasra-tayn = Fil	فِلٍ
Step 3	Join the two, = Uf-Fil	أُفْفِلٍ
Step 4	Laam, Fat-hah = La	لَ
Step 5	Join all previous, = Uf-Fil-La	أُفْفِلَ
Step 6	Kaaf, Meem, Dhammah = Koom	كُمْ
Step 7	Read the entire word, = Uf-Fil-La-Koom	أُفْفِلَكُمْ

If after a Noon Saakin or Tanween, the letters ل or ر appear, there will be Idghaam without Ghunnah.

QUICK TIPS

Idghaam without Ghunnah only happens when joining on to the letters 'Laam' ل and 'Ra' ر

CHECKLIST

☑ I can **read and spell** the words that include **Idghaam** fluently.

☑ I can read each line **fluently in one breath** (without hesitation or pausing).

☑ I can implement all the lessons learnt previously into this exercise.

LESSON 32 — IDGHAAM WITH GHUNNAH

اَنْ طَّمِسَ	لَنْ نَّبْرَحَ	مِنْ نَّفَادٍ	وَمَنْ نُّعَمِّرْهُ
مِنْ نَّذِيرٍ	مِنْ نُّطْفَةٍ	اَنْ نَّذِلَّ	مِنْ نَّبَاتٍ
حَظًّا مِّمَّا	عَدْلٍ مِّنْكُمْ	سِحْرٌ مُّبِينٌ	كِتَابًا مَّوْقُوتًا
نَبَإٍ مُّسْتَقَرٌّ	سُلْطَانًا مُّبِينًا	نَعِيمٌ مُّقِيمٌ	عَذَابًا مُّهِينًا
كُلٌّ يَّجْرِي	اَنْ يَّكْذِبُونَ	رَجُلٌ يُّرِيدُ	اَنْ يُّوقِعَ
شَأْنٌ يُّغْنِيهِ	مَنْ يُّؤْمِنْ	رِدْءًا يُّصَدِّقُنِي	مُنْقَلَبٍ يَّنْقَلِبُونَ
جَنَّتٍ وَّنَهَرٍ	مِنْ وَّرَثَتِ	سُجَّدًا وَّقِيَامًا	يَوْمَئِذٍ وَّاجِفَةٌ
سِرًّا وَّعَلَانِيَةً	زَجْرَةٌ وَّاحِدَةٌ	وَفَاكِهَةً وَّأَبًّا	اَمْنًا وَّاجْنُبْنِي

STEP BY STEP

➤ Read the words that include **Idghaam**
E.g. جِنَّتٌ وَّنَهَرٌ   كُلٌّ يَّجْرِى   حَطَامًا   اَنْ نَّطْمِسَ

➤ Spell the words which include a **Idghaam**. E.g.

Step 1	Alif, Noon, Fat-hah = An	اَنْ
Step 2	Noon, Taa, Fat-hah = Nat	نَّطْ
Step 3	Join the two, An-Nat	اَنْ نَّطْ
Step 4	Meem, Kasrah = Me	مِ
Step 5	Join all previous, An-Nat-Me	اَنْ نَّطْمِ
Step 6	Seen, Fat-hah = Sa	سَ
Step 7	Read the entire word, An-Nat-Me-Sa	اَنْ نَّطْمِسَ

If after a Noon Saakin or Tanween, the letters **و م ن ي** appear, there will be Idghaam with Ghunnah.

QUICK TIPS

➤ Remember this one word **Yarmaloon**, it has all the letters of Idghaam ي ر م ل و ن, which should help you remember them. **Ya-r-m-l-oo-n** = يَرْمَلُونَ

➤ Remember this one word **Yanmoo**, it has all the letters of Idghaam with Ghunnah و م ن ي, it should help you remember them. **Yanmoo** = يَنْمُو

CHECKLIST

☑ I can **read and spell** the words that include **Idghaam** fluently.

☑ I can read each line **fluently in one breath** (without hesitation or pausing).

☑ I can implement all the lessons learnt previously into this exercise.

GRADE 15

The Prophet ﷺ said:

"Read the Qur'aan regularly. By the One in Whose Hand Muhammad's soul is, it escapes from memory faster than a camel does from its tying ropes."

(Muslim)

OVERVIEW

LESSON 33 > **IKHFAA**

Ikhfaa is to stretch with a light nasal sound

- If after a **Noon Saakin** or **Tanween** any of the following 15 letters appear: ت ث ج د ذ ز س ش ص ض ط ظ ف ق ك the sound of the **Noon Saakin** or **Tanween** will be stretched in the nose similar to Ghunnah اَنْتُمْ.
- The difference between the two sounds is that in Ghunnah the tongue is flat when touching the upper palate (roof of the mouth) which makes a deep nasal sound. In Ikhfaa the tip of the tongue touches the upper palate which makes a lighter sound from the nose.

LESSON 34 > **MEEM SAAKIN**

Ikhfaa Meem Saakin is to stretch with a deep nasal sound

- If after a Meem Saakin the letter **Ba** ب or **Meem** م appears, there will be Ikhfaa لَهُمْ مَغْفِرَةٌ مِنْهُمْ يَظْلَمُ. If any other letter appears then the Meem Saakin will be read normally without any stretch.

LESSON 35 > **IQLAAB**

Iqlaab is to replace the Noon Saakin or Tanween with a small Meem

- If after a **Noon Saakin** or **Tanween** the letter **Ba** ب appears, the **Noon Saakin** will be replaced by a **small Meem** ذَنْبٍ.
- However, the **Tanween** will join straight onto the small Meem and will be read with a Ghunnah اَبَدًا بِهَا.

LESSON 36 > **NOON QUTNI**

Noon Qutni is a small Noon with a Kasrah

- If a **Noon Qutni** (small Noon) appears under an Alif, then ignore the Alif and read Noon as normal. However, if there is an **Alif before the Noon Qutni** (small Noon) then the Alif will be cancelled عَادَ الْأُوْلَىٰ.

LESSON 33 — IKHFAA

عِنْدَ

تُنْذِرُ	مِنْكُمْ	جُنْدٍ	اَنْتُمْ
مُنْقَلَبٌ	اَنْجُكُمْ	تَنْشَقُّ	اَنْفَقُوا
يَنْطِقُونَ	يَحْزُنْكَ	مَنْشُورًا	فَانْطَلَقَا
يَنْظُرُونَ	اَنْشَأْنَهُ	اَنْفُسَهُمْ	تَنْقُصُهَا
ذُرِّيَّةً ضِعَافًا	ثَمَنًا قَلِيلًا	مِنْ قَبْلُ	يَنْصُرُونَهُ
مِمَّنْ تَرْضَوْنَ	عَذَابًا شَدِيدًا	رِجَالًا كَثِيرًا	اَذًى كَثِيرًا
خَالِدًا فِيهَا	مِنْ قَبْلِكُمْ	لَنْ تُقَاتِلُوا	مِنْ فَضْلِهِ
وَاَنْفُسَنَا وَاَنْفُسَكُمْ	اَوْ قُتِلَ انْقَلَبْتُمْ	سُورَةٌ تُنَبِّئُهُمْ	مَرْجُوًّا قَبْلُ

STEP BY STEP

•▶ Read the words that include Ikhfaa.
E.g. Annn-tum أَنْتُمْ , Junnn-din جُنْدٍ , Minnn-kum مِنْكُمْ .

•▶ Spell the words that include Ikhfaa (refer to Lesson 06: Sukoon).

•▶ Identify and apply Ikhfaa properly.

If after a Noon Saakin or Tanween any of these fifteen letters appear ت ث ج د ذ ز س ش ص ض ط ظ ف ق ك there will be a stretch with a light nasal sound.

QUICK TIPS

There are 2 ways to learn the Ikhfaa letters:
1) By elimination: After excluding the Ba, Izhaar & Idghaam letters, you are left with the Ikhfaa letters. OR
2) Memorising: Memorise the Ikhfaa letters and try to say them under 5 seconds.

CHECKLIST

☑ I can **read and spell** the words that include Ikhfaa.

☑ I can read each line **fluently in one breath** (without hesitation or pausing).

☑ I can implement all the lessons learnt previously into this exercise.

LESSON 34: MEEM SAAKIN

هُمْ بَطْ

مِنْهُمْ بَطْشًا	لَهُمْ مَغْفِرَةٌ	سَبَقَكُمْ بِهَا	فَهُمْ مُسْلِمُونَ
نَمْلَةٌ	تَمْشِي	أَتْمَمْتَ	أَمْوَالِهِمْ
لَهُمْ قَوْلًا	بَعْضُكُمْ بَعْضًا	بِهِمْ مُؤْمِنُونَ	وَهُمْ مُهْتَدُونَ
لَكُمْ فَتْحٌ	يَأْتِيكُمْ بِلَيْلٍ	أَخَاهُمْ صَالِحًا	أَنْتُمْ مُطَّلِعُونَ
وَمِثْلَهُمْ مَعَهُمْ	أَعْمَالَهُمْ فِيهَا	فَأَمْسِكُوهُنَّ	أَنْتُمْ بِمُعْجِزِينَ
أَذَاقَهُمْ مِنْهُ	لَهُمْ لَا تَعُدُّوا	فَهُمْ مُقْمَحُونَ	كُنْتُمْ مُجْرِمِينَ
فَهُمْ يُوزَعُونَ	لَمْ يُفِرُّوا	مِنْهُمْ مُقْتَصِدٌ	وَاضْمُمْ إِلَيْكَ
كُنْتُمْ مَرْضَى	دَخَلْتُمْ بِهِنَّ	أَصَبْتُمْ مِثْلَيْهَا	فَلَكُمْ رُءُوسُ

- ▸ Read the words that include Ikhfaa and Izhaar.
  E.g. Ikhfaa: Minhummm-batshan مِنْهُمْ بَطْشًا ,
  Izhaar: Namlatun نَمْلَةٌ .

- ▸ Spell the words that include Ikhfaa and Izhaar.
  (refer to Lesson 06: Sukoon)

If after a Meem Saakin مْ the letters ب or م appear, then there will be a stretch on the Meem Saakin with a deep nasal sound.

The only 2 letters to remember after the Meem Saakin are: **Ba and Meem**.

- ✓ I can **read and spell** the words that include **Ikhfaa** and **Izhaar** fluently.

- ✓ I can read each line **fluently in one breath** (without hesitation or pausing).

- ✓ I can implement all the lessons learnt previously into this exercise.

LESSON 35 — IQLAAB

يَنْۢبَغِي	فَاَنْۢبِذْ	اَنْۢبَآءُ	ذَنْۢبٍ
زَوْجٍۭ بَهِيجٍ	وَاقِعٌۢ بِهِمْ	عَلِيْمٌۢ بِهٖ	اَبَدًاۢ بِمَا
مَنْۢ بَخِلَ	مِنْۢ بَابٍ	لَيُنْۢبَذَنَّ	مِنْۢ بَيْنِ
مَكَانٍۭ بَعِيْدٍ	جُدَدٌۢ بِيْضٌ	بِالْجَنْۢبِ	سُنْۢبُلَتٍ
بِثَمَنٍۭ بَخْسٍ	وَضَآئِقٌۢ بِهٖ	سَوَآءٌۢ بَيْنَنَا	مُنْۢفَطِرٌۢ بِهٖ
سَيِّئَةٍۭ بِمِثْلِهَا	سُلْطَانٍۭ بِهٰذَا	قَرْيَةٍۭ بَطِرَتْ	كُلًّاۢ بِسِيْمٰهُمْ
لَيًّاۢ بِاَلْسِنَتِهِمْ	قَآئِمًاۢ بِالْقِسْطِ	مُصَدِّقًاۢ بِكَلِمَةٍ	بَصِيْرٌۢ بِالْعِبَادِ
اخُذْۢ بِنَاصِيَتِهَا	اَوْدِيَةٌۢ بِقَدَرِهَا	مُؤَذِّنٌۢ بَيْنَهُمْ	وَيَسْتَنْۢبِئُوْنَكَ

STEP BY STEP

→ Read the words that include Iqlaab.
E.g. Thamm-bin ذَنۢبٍ , Ammbaaaaa-e اَنۢبَآءِ , Famm-bith فَاَنۢبِذۡ .

→ Spell the words which include Iqlaab.
E.g.

Step 1	Thaal, Meem, Fat-hah = Tham	ذَمَّ
Step 2	Ba, Kasrah-tayn = Bin	بٍ
Step 3	Read the entire word, Tham-Bin	ذَنۢبٍ

If after a Noon Saakin or Tanween the letter Ba ب appears, the Noon Saakin and Tanween will be replaced with a small Meem ࢧ .

QUICK TIPS

When joining onto the small Meem always make a stretched nasal sound.

CHECKLIST

✓ I can **read and spell** the words that include **Iqlaab** fluently.

✓ I can read each line **fluently in one breath** (without hesitation or pausing.)

✓ I can implement all the lessons learnt previously into this exercise.

LESSON 36 — NOON QUTNI نْ

خَيْرُ الْوَصِيَّةُ	قَدِيرٌ الَّذِى	عَادٌ الْأُولَى	نُوحٌ ابْنَهُ
لَهْوٌ انْفَضُّوا	شِيَبًا السَّمَاءُ	لُمَزَةٍ الَّذِى	نَذِيرٌ الَّذِى
جَمِيعًا الَّذِى	فَخُورٌ الَّذِينَ	رَجُلٌ افْتَرَى	خَبِيرًا الَّذِى
شَكُورٌ الَّذِى	مُرْتَابٌ الَّذِينَ	يَوْمَئِذٍ الْحَقُّ	إِفْكٌ افْتَرَاهُ
نُفُورًا اسْتِكْبَارًا	بِزِينَةٍ الْكَوَاكِبِ	عَادٌ الْمُرْسَلِينَ	يَوْمَئِذٍ الْمُسْتَقَرُّ
مَقْدُورًا الَّذِينَ	لُوطٍ الْمُرْسَلِينَ	شَيْئًا تَخَذْنَهَا	نُوحٌ الْمُرْسَلِينَ
رَهْبَانِيَّةً ابْتَدَعُوهَا	وَأَمْوَالٌ اقْتَرَفْتُمُوهَا	مَثَلَ الْقَوْمِ الَّذِينَ	
قَوْمًا اللهُ مُهْلِكُهُمْ	إِلَى بَعْضِ الْقَوْلِ	جَنَّاتِ عَدْنٍ الَّتِى	

 Completed on D D / M M / YEAR

STEP BY STEP

- Read the words that include a Noon Qutni without spelling. E.g. Noo-hu-nib-na-hoo نُوْحٌ اِبْنَهُ , Aa-da-nil-oolaa عَادًا الْأُوْلَى .

- Spell the words which include a Noon Qutni. E.g.

Step 1	Noon, Waw, Dhammah = Noo	نُوْ
Step 2	Ha, Dhammah = Hu	حُ
Step 3	Join the two, Noo-Hu	نُوْحُ
Step 4	Noon, Ba, Kasrah = Nib	اِبْ
Step 5	Join all previous, Noo-Hu-Nib	نُوْحُ اِبْ
Step 6	Noon, Fat-hah = Na	نَ
Step 7	Join all previous, Noo-Hu-Nib-Na	نُوْحُ اِبْنَ
Step 8	Ha, Madd Dhammah = Hoo	هُ
Step 9	Read the entire word, Noo-Hu-Nib-Na-Hoo	نُوْحٌ اِبْنَهُ

If an Alif comes before a small Noon ڻ it will be ignored.

Read the Noon Qutni as a normal Noon with a Kasrah. However if an Alif appears before the Noon Qutni, the Alif will be ignored.

QUICK TIPS

CHECKLIST

- I can **read and spell** the words that include a Noon Qutni fluently.
- I can read each line **fluently in one breath** (without hesitation or pausing).
- I can implement all the lessons learnt previously into this exercise.

Comments

GRADE 16

The Prophet ﷺ said:

"Any group of people that assemble in one of the Houses of Allaah to recite the Book of Allaah, learning and teaching it, tranquility will descend upon them, mercy will engulf them, Angels will surround them and Allaah will make mention of them to those (the angels) in His proximity."

[Muslim]

OVERVIEW

 **LESSON 37** > **STOPPING ON ROUND TA (TA MARBOOTAH)**

- When stopping on a **Taa Marbootah** ة the Taa will be **replaced** by a **Haa Saakin** هْ regardless of the Harakah on the Taa.

LESSON 38 > **STOPPING ON FAT-HA-TAYN**

- If the last letter has a **Fat-ha-tayn** and an **Alif** e.g. رًا : Fat-ha-tayn will be **replaced** with a **Fat-hah** رَ.
- **Fat-ha-tayn without an Alif** after it e.g. ءٍ : Fat-ha-tayn will be **replaced** by a **Fat-hah** followed by an **Alif** ءَا.

LESSON 39 > **WAQF (STOPPING)**

- **Nothing changes If:** The last letter is a Saakin letter كُمْ or Fat-hah followed by an Alif هَا or Madd Fat-hah نِى.
- **Shaddah:** If the last letter has a Shaddah on it يِّ, then the Shaddah will remain but the Harakah will be silenced يِّْ.
- **Everything else:** (Leaving aside the Taa Marbootah, Fat-ha-tayn and the rules learnt above), if any other Harakah appears on the last letter فَقَتَلَهُ, the Harakah will be replaced by a Sukoon فَقَتَلَهْ.

LESSON 40 > **WAQF (STOPPING)**

- Ensure all previous **Tajweed** rules are exercised in this lesson.

LESSON 41 > **SAKTAH & WAQFAH**

- **Saktah** سكتة and **Waqfah** وقفة is to pause the recitation without taking a breath for a second, then continue to read رَاقٍ ۜ مَنْ وَقِيلَ.
- There are four places in the Qur'aan where Saktah is compulsory, they have been coloured in red.

LESSON 37: STOPPING ON 'TA' MARBOOTAH

مِنْهُمْ تُقٰةً ○	كُتُبٌ قَيِّمَةٌ ○	مَثَلُ الْجَنَّةِ ○
ذُرِّيَّةً طَيِّبَةً ○	وَأَقِمِ الصَّلٰوةَ ○	وَفَاكِهَةٍ كَثِيرَةٍ ○
أَهْلِ الْمَدِينَةِ ○	حَيٰوةً طَيِّبَةً ○	تَحْتَ الشَّجَرَةِ ○
أَمْ بِهٖ جِنَّةٌ ○	سُورَةٌ مُّحْكَمَةٌ ○	وَهُدًى وَرَحْمَةٌ ○
فِي جَنَّةٍ عَالِيَةٍ ○	وَمَغَانِمَ كَثِيرَةً ○	كَمَا لَهُمْ اٰلِهَةٌ ○
ٱلْأَرْضُ الْمَيْتَةُ ○	أَصْحَابَ الْقَرْيَةِ ○	إِذَا دَعَاكُمْ دَعْوَةً ○
أَعِظْكُمْ بِوَاحِدَةٍ ○	ظَاهِرَةً وَبَاطِنَةً ○	وُجُوهُهُمْ مُّسْوَدَّةٌ ○
ضَاحِكَةٌ مُّسْتَبْشِرَةٌ ○	فِي قُلُوبِهِمُ الْحَمِيَّةَ ○	وَتُسَبِّحُوهُ بُكْرَةً ○

   Completed on / /

STEP BY STEP

•▶ Apply Waqf correctly on words that end with the **round Ta (Ta Marbootah)**.

Before Waqf	After Waqf
مَثَلُ الْجَنَّةِ ○	مَثَلُ الْجَنَّهْ ○
كُتُبٌ قَيِّمَةٌ ○	كُتُبٌ قَيِّمَهْ ○
مِنْهُمْ ثُقَةٌ ○	مِنْهُمْ ثُقَهْ ○

QUICK TIPS

When stopping on a **Round Ta** ة , it will always be replaced with a **Ha** هْ **Saakin**.

CHECKLIST

✓ I can read and apply Waqf on **Ta Marbootah** fluently.

✓ I can read each line **fluently and quickly**.

✓ I can implement all the lessons learnt previously into this exercise.

LESSON 38: STOPPING ON FAT-HA-TAYN

بَشَرًا رَّسُولًا	رَبِّ رَضِيًّا	خِطْأً كَبِيرًا
سُجَّدًا وَّبُكِيًّا	صَعِيدًا زَلَقًا	بُكْرَةً وَّعَشِيًّا
بَيْنَكُمْ شَهِيدًا	رَسُولًا نَّبِيًّا	مَكَانًا عَلِيًّا
وَكَبِّرْهُ تَكْبِيرًا	وَلِيًّا مُّرْشِدًا	أَقْرَبَ رُحْمًا
أُبْعَثُ حَيًّا	تَحْتَكِ سَرِيًّا	رُطَبًا جَنِيًّا
غُلَامًا زَكِيًّا	مَكَانًا شَرْقِيًّا	صِرَاطًا سَوِيًّا
يُحْسِنُونَ صُنْعًا	وَنَزَّلْنَهُ تَنْزِيلًا	اِلَى أَجَلٍ مُّسَمًّى
أَوْ أَمْضِيَ حُقُبًا	وَازْدَادُوا تِسْعًا	وَأَضْعَفُ جُنْدًا

▸ Read and apply the **Waqf** on **Fat-ha-tayn** correctly. E.g.

Before Waqf	After Waqf
○ خِطْأً كَبِيرًا	○ خِطْأً كَبِيرًا
○ رَبِّ رَضِيًّا	○ رَبِّ رَضِيًّا
○ بَشَرًا رَسُولًا	○ بَشَرًا رَسُولًا

When stopping on a Fat-ha-tayn ـًا remove one Fat-hah. You should be left with a Fat-hah followed by an Alif ـَا .

✓ I can apply **Waqf on Fat-ha-tayn** fluently.

✓ I can read **each line fluently** (without hesitation or pausing).

✓ I can implement all the lessons learnt previously into this exercise.

LESSON 39 — WAQF

○ وَأَوْفُوا بِالْعَهْدِ	○ رُدُّوهَا عَلَيَّ	○ أَغْنَىٰ وَأَقْنَىٰ
○ أَسْمِعْ بِهِمْ	○ عَلَّمَ الْقُرْآنَ	○ رَبُّ الْمَشْرِقَيْنِ
○ ذَٰلِكَ وَأَصْلَحُوا	○ كَذِبًا أَمْرِهِ	○ وَرَفَعْنَا لَكَ ذِكْرَكَ
○ رَبِّ أَكْرَمَنِ	○ فَقَالَ أَكْفِلْنِيهَا	○ غُلَامًا فَقَتَلَهُ
○ وَأَدْبَارَ السُّجُودِ	○ وَنَأْىٰ بِجَانِبِهِ	○ وَبَرًّا بِوَالِدَتِي
○ آتَيْتَهُنَّ كُلَّهُنَّ	○ هَاجَرْنَ مَعَكَ	○ وَحْيٌ يُوحَىٰ
○ شَاكِرًا لِأَنْعُمِهِ	○ خَشْيَةَ الْإِنْفَاقِ	○ وَتَرَبَّصْتُمْ وَارْتَبْتُمْ
○ قِسْمَةٌ ضِيزَىٰ	○ قِيلَ ارْجِعُوا وَرَاءَكُمْ	○ اقْرَأْ وَرَبُّكَ الْأَكْرَمُ

   Completed on   /   /

STEP BY STEP

• Apply **Waqf** correctly. E.g.

Before Waqf	After Waqf
○ وَأَوْفُوا بِالْعَهْدِ	○ وَأَوْفُوا بِالْعَهْدْ
○ رُدُّوهَا عَلَىَّ	○ رُدُّوهَا عَلَىَّ
○ أَغْنَى وَأَقْنَى	○ أَغْنَى وَأَقْنَى

When applying Waqf the last letter will be given a Sukoon unless some of the following appear on the last letter: Ta Marbootah ةً , Fat-hah-tayn اً , Madd Fathah ىٰ , Fat-hah followed by an Alif هَا , Shaddah عَلَىَّ .

QUICK TIPS

Does change		
ةْ	=	ةً
رْا	=	رًا
يْ	=	يَّ
فَقْتَلَهْ	=	فَقْتَلَهُ

Does not change		
كُمْ	=	كُمْ
هَا	=	هَا
نٰى	=	نٰى

CHECKLIST

✓ I can **read and spell** the words that include **Waqf** fluently.
✓ I can read and apply **Waqf** correctly.
✓ I can implement all the lessons learnt previously into this exercise.

Lesson 40: WAQF ON THREE WORDS

اِلٰهُكُمُ اللّٰهُ وَاحِدٌ ○	اَنِ اعْبُدُوا اللّٰهَ ○	ءَاِلٰهٌ مَّعَ اللّٰهِ ○
عَلَّمَهُ شَدِيدُ الْقُوٰى ○	ثُمَّ اَدْبَرَ وَاسْتَكْبَرَ ○	نُوْرٌ عَلٰى نُوْرٍ ○
وَاللّٰهُ وَاسِعٌ عَلِيْمٌ ○	اَفَغَيْرَ اللّٰهِ تَتَّقُوْنَ ○	قُمِ الَّيْلَ اِلَّا قَلِيْلًا ○
وَتَسِيْرُ الْجِبَالُ سَيْرًا ○	لَا يَمَسُّهُ اِلَّا الْمُطَهَّرُوْنَ ○	وَكُنْتُمْ اَزْوَاجًا ثَلٰثَةً ○
وَلَنِعْمَ دَارُ الْمُتَّقِيْنَ ○	فَشٰرِبُوْنَ شُرْبَ الْهِيْمِ ○	عِنْدَ سِدْرَةِ الْمُنْتَهٰى ○
وَلَاَجْرُ الْاٰخِرَةِ اَكْبَرُ ○	يَخْلُقُ اللّٰهُ مَا يَشَاءُ ○	اَفْتَرُوْنَهُ عَلٰى مَا يَرٰى ○
اِنِّيْ اَنَا النَّذِيْرُ الْمُبِيْنُ ○	وَجَعَلَ الشَّمْسَ سِرَاجًا ○	اِذَا رُجَّتِ الْاَرْضُ رَجًّا ○
فَلَا اُقْسِمُ بِمَوَاقِعِ النُّجُوْمِ ○	قِيْلَ لَهَا ادْخُلِى الصَّرْحَ ○	كَاَنَّهُمْ حُمُرٌ مُسْتَنْفِرَةٌ ○

    Completed on   /   /

STEP BY STEP

▸ Apply Waqf correctly. E.g.

Before Waqf	After Waqf
○ عَاِلهَ مَّعَ اللّٰهِ	○ عَاِلهَ مَّعَ اللّٰهْ
○ اَنِ اعْبُدُوا اللّٰهَ	○ اَنِ اعْبُدُوا اللّٰهْ
○ اِلْهُكُمُ اللّٰهُ وَاحِدٌ	○ اِلْهُكُمُ اللّٰهُ وَاحِدْ

When applying Waqf the last letter will be given a Sukoon unless some of the following appear on the last letter: Ta Marbootah ة , Fat-hah-tayn اً , Madd Fathah رَى , Fat-hah followed by an Alif هَا , Shaddah عَدٌّ .

QUICK TIPS

Does change			Does not change		
ةً	=	ه	كُمْ	=	كُمْ
رَا	=	رَا	هَا	=	هَا
يُّ	=	يُّ	نِّي	=	نِّي
فَقْتَلَهْ	=	فَقْتَلَهُ			

CHECKLIST

- ✓ I can **read and spell** the words that include **Waqf** fluently.
- ✓ I can read and apply **Waqf** correctly.
- ✓ I can implement all the lessons learnt previously into this exercise.

LESSON 41 — SAKTAH AND WAQFAH

سكتة

وَقِيلَ مَنْ ۜسكتة رَاقٍ	عِوَجًا ۜسكتة قَيِّمًا لِّيُنذِرَ
مِن مَّرْقَدِنَا ۜسكتة هَٰذَا مَا وَعَدَ الرَّحْمَٰنُ	كَلَّا بَلْ ۜسكتة رَانَ عَلَىٰ قُلُوبِهِم
أَعْلَمُ بِمَن فِيهَا ۜوقفة لَنُنَجِّيَنَّهُ	يُصْدِرَ الرِّعَاءُ ۜسكتة وَأَبُونَا شَيْخٌ كَبِيرٌ
أَنفُسَنَا ۜوقفة وَإِن لَّمْ تَغْفِرْ لَنَا	ٱلْحَيَوٰةُ ٱلدُّنْيَا ۜوقفة وَلَا يَغُرَّنَّكُمْ

STEP BY STEP

•▶ Read the words that include a Saktah and Waqfah without any hesitation. E.g.

وَقِيْلَ مَنْ ۜ رَاقٍ   وَإِنْ لَّمْ تَغْفِرْ لَنَا ۛ اَنْفُسَنَا

عِوَجًا ۜ قَيِّمًا لِّيُنْذِرَ   وَلَا يَغُرَّنَّكُمُ ۛ الْحَيٰوةُ الدُّنْيَا

QUICK TIPS

You pause without taking a breath and then continue. It's like a comma in English.

CHECKLIST

✓ I can **read and spell** the words that include **Saktah and Waqfah** fluently.

✓ I can read each part **in one breath** and applying **Saktah and Waqfah** correctly.

✓ I can implement all the lessons learnt previously into this exercise.

Comments

GRADE 17

The Prophet ﷺ said:

"The best amongst you is he who learns the Qur'an and teaches it to others."

(Bukhaari)

OVERVIEW

| LESSON 42 | > | ADVANCE STOPPING AND SAJDAH | |  |

- This symbol will always come in pairs in a verse, you'll **stop at one** and **carry on** at the other. The choice is yours. Do not stop at both and do not carry on without stopping on one of them.
- When a line comes above a word you must do a Sajdah Tilaawah at the end of that verse (Ayah).
  Note: *This line* *indicates where the Sajdah is and this word* *at the end of the verse (Ayah) indicates that Sajdah needs to be done.*

| LESSON 43 | > | HUROOF AL-MUQATTA'AAT | |  |

- Here we read the letter rather than the sound and stretch it according to the symbol on top of it. These letters are an exception to the general rule.
  For example: Nooooon , Qaaaaaf .
- By this stage the student should be familiar with all the **Waqf rules** and previous lessons.

| LESSON 44 | > | WAQF (STOPPING) | |  |

- When you read the longer verses and run out of breath, wherever you stop mid sentence, you will still need to apply the waqf rule. Then simply resume the recitation from one or two words before where the Waqf was applied.
- By this stage the student should be familiar with all the Spellings, Tajweed and Waqf rules.

م	Compulsory stop
ط ◯	Necessary stop
ج	Optional (stop or continue)
قف	Recommended pause
لا	Necessary to continue

LESSON 42: ADVANCE STOPPING AND SAJDAH

اِنَّ شَجَرَتَ الزَّقُّوْمِ ۙ طَعَامُ الْاَثِيْمِ ۛ كَالْمُهْلِ ۚ يَغْلِيْ فِي الْبُطُوْنِ ۙ وَاَنْفِقُوْا فِيْ سَبِيْلِ اللّٰهِ وَلَا تُلْقُوْا بِاَيْدِيْكُمْ اِلَى التَّهْلُكَةِ ۛ وَاَحْسِنُوْا ۚ اِنَّ اللّٰهَ يُحِبُّ الْمُحْسِنِيْنَ ۙ

فَاِمَّا مَنًّۢا بَعْدُ وَاِمَّا فِدَآءً حَتّٰى تَضَعَ الْحَرْبُ اَوْزَارَهَا ۛ ذٰلِكَ ۚ وَلَوْ يَشَآءُ اللّٰهُ لَانْتَصَرَ مِنْهُمْ ۙ وَقَالَ الَّذِيْنَ كَفَرُوْا لَوْلَا نُزِّلَ عَلَيْهِ الْقُرْاٰنُ جُمْلَةً وَّاحِدَةً ۛ

كَذٰلِكَ ۛ لِنُثَبِّتَ بِهٖ فُؤَادَكَ وَرَتَّلْنٰهُ تَرْتِيْلًا ۙ

السجدة
كَلَّا لَا تُطِعْهُ وَاسْجُدْ وَاقْتَرِبْ ۩

السجدة
وَاِذَا قُرِئَ عَلَيْهِمُ الْقُرْاٰنُ لَا يَسْجُدُوْنَ ۩

السجدة
اِنَّمَا يُؤْمِنُ بِاٰيٰتِنَا الَّذِيْنَ اِذَا ذُكِّرُوْا بِهَا خَرُّوْا سُجَّدًا

السجدة
وَّسَبَّحُوْا بِحَمْدِ رَبِّهِمْ وَهُمْ لَا يَسْتَكْبِرُوْنَ ۩

STEP BY STEP

• Read the Ayah (sentences) correctly and fluently.
• Learn all the Advanced Waqf and Sajdah rules properly.

مـ		Compulsory stop
ط	◯	Necessary stop
ج		Optional (stop or continue)
قف		Recommended pause
لا		Necessary to continue

QUICK TIPS

• ∴ = Stop at one and carry on at the other.
• وَاسْجُدْ = Sajdah is compulsory.

CHECKLIST

☑ I can apply **Advance Waqf and Sajdah** properly.

☑ I can read each part in **one breath** correctly.

☑ I can implement all the lessons learnt previously into this exercise.

LESSON 43: HUROOF AL-MUQATTA'AAT

يسٓ

قٓ	نٓ	صٓ	طه
يسٓ	حمٓ	طسٓ	الٓمٓرٰ
طسمٓ	عسٓقٓ	الٓمٓصٓ	كهيعصٓ

COMPLETE VERSE FLUENCY

حمٓ ۞ عسٓقٓ ۞ كَذٰلِكَ يُوْحِىٓ اِلَيْكَ وَاِلَى الَّذِيْنَ مِنْ قَبْلِكَ ۙ

اللّٰهُ الْعَزِيْزُ الْحَكِيْمُ ۞ الٓمٓرٰ ۫ تِلْكَ اٰيٰتُ الْكِتٰبِ ۞ كهيعصٓ ۞

ذِكْرُ رَحْمَتِ رَبِّكَ عَبْدَهٗ زَكَرِيَّا ۞ يسٓ ۞ وَالْقُرْاٰنِ الْحَكِيْمِ ۞

حمٓ ۚ تَنْزِيْلٌ مِّنَ الرَّحْمٰنِ الرَّحِيْمِ ۚ كِتٰبٌ فُصِّلَتْ اٰيٰتُهٗ قُرْاٰنًا عَرَبِيًّا

لِّقَوْمٍ يَّعْلَمُوْنَ ۞ وَلَا تَحْسَبَنَّ الَّذِيْنَ قُتِلُوْا فِيْ سَبِيْلِ اللّٰهِ اَمْوَاتًا ۚ

بَلْ اَحْيَآءٌ عِنْدَ رَبِّهِمْ يُرْزَقُوْنَ ۞ الٓرٰ ۫ تِلْكَ اٰيٰتُ الْكِتٰبِ الْحَكِيْمِ ۞

- Read the **Haroof Al-Muqatta'aat** correctly. E.g.: "Qaaaaaf" قٓ, "Nooooon" نٓ, "Saaaaad" صٓ

- Spell the Haroof Al-Muqatta'aat. E.g.

| Step 1 | Qaaf-Madd "Qaaaaaf" | قٓ |

- Identify the Haroof Al-Muqatta'aat. They only come at the beginning of certain Surahs.

- You only say the letters and then stretch them depending on the type of Madd.

- I can **read and spell** the Haroof Al-Muqatta'aat.
- I can read each line **fluently and quickly**.
- I can implement all the lessons learnt previously into this exercise.

LESSON 44 — COMPLETE VERSE FLUENCY

وَقُلِ الْحَقُّ مِن رَّبِّكُمْ ۖ فَمَن شَآءَ فَلْيُؤْمِن وَّمَن شَآءَ فَلْيَكْفُرْ ۚ اِنَّآ اَعْتَدْنَا لِلظّٰلِمِينَ نَارًا ۙ اَحَاطَ بِهِمْ سُرَادِقُهَا ۚ وَاِن يَّسْتَغِيثُوْا يُغَاثُوْا بِمَآءٍ كَالْمُهْلِ يَشْوِى الْوُجُوْهَ ۚ بِئْسَ الشَّرَابُ ۗ وَسَآءَتْ مُرْتَفَقًا ۞ يٰزَكَرِيَّآ اِنَّا نُبَشِّرُكَ بِغُلٰمِ ِاسْمُهُ يَحْيٰى ۙ لَمْ نَجْعَل لَّهُ مِن قَبْلُ سَمِيًّا ۞ يٰيَحْيٰى خُذِ الْكِتٰبَ بِقُوَّةٍ ۖ وَاٰتَيْنٰهُ الْحُكْمَ صَبِيًّا ۞ وَاذْكُرْ فِى الْكِتٰبِ مَرْيَمَ ۘ اِذِ انْتَبَذَتْ مِنْ اَهْلِهَا مَكَانًا شَرْقِيًّا ۞ قَالَ كَذٰلِكِ ۚ قَالَ رَبُّكِ هُوَ عَلَىَّ هَيِّنٌ ۚ وَلِنَجْعَلَهُ اٰيَةً لِّلنَّاسِ وَرَحْمَةً مِّنَّا ۚ وَكَانَ اَمْرًا مَّقْضِيًّا ۞ هَلْ اَتٰىكَ حَدِيْثُ ضَيْفِ اِبْرٰهِيْمَ الْمُكْرَمِيْنَ ۘ وَهَلْ اَتٰىكَ نَبَؤُا الْخَصْمِ ۘ اِذْ تَسَوَّرُوا الْمِحْرَابَ ۞

- Identify and apply all the Tajweed rules from Grade 12 onwards properly.
- Identify and apply Waqf properly.

م	Compulsory stop
ط ◯	Necessary stop
ج	Optional (stop or continue)
قف	Recommended pause
لا	Necessary to continue

QUICK TIPS

Read at a medium pace without stretching Fat-hah, Kasrah and Dhammah.
When you come across a Noon Saakin or Tanween lookout for a Tajweed rule.

CHECKLIST

- ✓ I can **read with Tajweed** by myself.
- ✓ I can read each Ayah (verse) fluently in one breath.
- ✓ I can read the entire Qaa'idah before progressing onto the Qur'aan.

LESSON 44
COMPLETE VERSE FLUENCY

قَدْ صَدَّقْتَ الرُّءْيَا ۚ اِنَّا كَذٰلِكَ نَجْزِى الْمُحْسِنِيْنَ ۞ اِنَّهُمْ كَانُوْۤا

اِذَا قِيْلَ لَهُمْ لَاۤ اِلٰهَ اِلَّا اللّٰهُ ۙ يَسْتَكْبِرُوْنَ ۞ فَفِرُّوْۤا اِلَى اللّٰهِ ۚ

اِنِّىْ لَكُمْ مِّنْهُ نَذِيْرٌ ۞ اَللّٰهُ لَاۤ اِلٰهَ اِلَّا هُوَ ۚ لَهُ الْاَسْمَآءُ الْحُسْنٰى ۞

وَهَلْ اَتٰىكَ حَدِيْثُ مُوْسٰى ۘ اَتَوَاصَوْا بِهٖ ۚ بَلْ هُمْ قَوْمٌ طَاغُوْنَ ۞

اَمْ خَلَقُوا السَّمٰوٰتِ وَالْاَرْضَ ۚ بَلْ لَّا يُوْقِنُوْنَ ۞ سَخَّرَهَا عَلَيْهِمْ

سَبْعَ لَيَالٍ وَّثَمٰنِيَةَ اَيَّامٍ ۙ حُسُوْمًا ۙ فَتَرَى الْقَوْمَ فِيْهَا صَرْعٰى ۙ

كَاَنَّهُمْ اَعْجَازُ نَخْلٍ خَاوِيَةٍ ۞ وَلَهٗ مَنْ فِى السَّمٰوٰتِ وَالْاَرْضِ ۚ

كُلٌّ لَّهٗ قٰنِتُوْنَ ۞ قُلُوْبٌ يَّوْمَئِذٍ وَّاجِفَةٌ ۙ اَبْصَارُهَا خَاشِعَةٌ ۘ

اَمْ حَسِبْتَ اَنَّ اَصْحٰبَ الْكَهْفِ وَالرَّقِيْمِ ۙ كَانُوْا مِنْ اٰيٰتِنَا عَجَبًا ۞

Apply the following correctly:

- Qalqalah
- Ghunnah
- Izhaar
- Ra rule
- Word of Allaah rule
- Idghaam
- Ikhfaa
- Meem Saakin
- Iqlaab
- Noon Qutni
- Saktah and Waqfah
- Waqf on "Ta" Marbootah
- Waqf on Fat-ha-tayn
- Waqf

QUICK TIPS

Read as fast as possible without stretching Fat-hah, Kasrah and Dhammah.

CHECKLIST

- I can **read with Tajweed** by myself.
- I can read each Ayah (verse) **fluently in one breath** (without hesitation or pausing).
- I can read the entire Qaa'idah before progressing onto the Qur'aan.

GRADE 18

The Prophet ﷺ said:

"He who does not memorise any part from the Qur'an he is like the ruined house."

(Tirmidhi)

OVERVIEW

LESSON 45 > **MEMORISATION OF THE LAST 10 SURAHS**

- Every student must learn the last 10 Surahs from memory with the correct pronunciation ensuring all Tajweed rules are applied properly.
- These Surahs are normally read during prayers as they are short and easy to learn. It is very important to memorise at least a portion of the Qur'aan so that Allaah may shower His mercy upon us.

ﻡ	Compulsory stop
ط ◯	Necessary stop
ج	Optional (stop or continue)
قف	Recommended pause
لا	Necessary to continue

FINAL > **STUDENT CHECKLIST**

- Every student should go through the checklist and check that they are confident in all the lessons that they have learnt.

LESSON 45
LAST 10 SURAHS

بِسْمِ اللهِ الرَّحْمٰنِ الرَّحِيْمِ

اَلْحَمْدُ لِلّٰهِ رَبِّ الْعٰلَمِيْنَ ۙ الرَّحْمٰنِ الرَّحِيْمِ ۙ مٰلِكِ يَوْمِ الدِّيْنِ ۭ اِيَّاكَ نَعْبُدُ وَاِيَّاكَ نَسْتَعِيْنُ ۭ اِهْدِنَا الصِّرَاطَ الْمُسْتَقِيْمَ ۙ صِرَاطَ الَّذِيْنَ اَنْعَمْتَ عَلَيْهِمْ ۙ غَيْرِ الْمَغْضُوْبِ عَلَيْهِمْ وَلَا الضَّآلِّيْنَ ۧ

بِسْمِ اللهِ الرَّحْمٰنِ الرَّحِيْمِ

قُلْ اَعُوْذُ بِرَبِّ النَّاسِ ۙ مَلِكِ النَّاسِ ۙ اِلٰهِ النَّاسِ ۙ مِنْ شَرِّ الْوَسْوَاسِ الْخَنَّاسِ ۙ الَّذِيْ يُوَسْوِسُ فِيْ صُدُوْرِ النَّاسِ ۙ مِنَ الْجِنَّةِ وَالنَّاسِ ۧ

بِسْمِ اللهِ الرَّحْمٰنِ الرَّحِيْمِ

قُلْ اَعُوْذُ بِرَبِّ الْفَلَقِ ۙ مِنْ شَرِّ مَا خَلَقَ ۙ وَمِنْ شَرِّ غَاسِقٍ اِذَا وَقَبَ ۙ وَمِنْ شَرِّ النَّفّٰثٰتِ فِي الْعُقَدِ ۙ وَمِنْ شَرِّ حَاسِدٍ اِذَا حَسَدَ ۧ

بِسْمِ اللهِ الرَّحْمٰنِ الرَّحِيْمِ

قُلْ هُوَ اللهُ اَحَدٌ ۙ اَللهُ الصَّمَدُ ۙ لَمْ يَلِدْ ۙ وَلَمْ يُوْلَدْ ۙ وَلَمْ يَكُنْ لَّهٗ كُفُوًا اَحَدٌ ۧ

   Completed on / /

•▶ Read and memorise the Surahs.

Read one verse repeatedly to help memorise, then the next verse repeatedly. Join the two verses to test yourselves. Keep doing this until you learn the whole Surah.

- I can read the **Surahs from memory** fluently.
- I can implement all the lessons learnt previously into this exercise.

Comments

LESSON 45 — LAST 10 SURAHS

بِسْمِ اللهِ الرَّحْمٰنِ الرَّحِيْمِ

تَبَّتْ يَدَآ أَبِىْ لَهَبٍ وَّتَبَّ ۚ مَآ أَغْنٰى عَنْهُ مَالُهٗ وَمَا كَسَبَ ۚ سَيَصْلٰى نَارًا ذَاتَ لَهَبٍ ۚ وَّامْرَاَتُهٗ ۚ حَمَّالَةَ الْحَطَبِ ۚ فِىْ جِيْدِهَا حَبْلٌ مِّنْ مَّسَدٍ ۚ

بِسْمِ اللهِ الرَّحْمٰنِ الرَّحِيْمِ

اِذَا جَآءَ نَصْرُ اللهِ وَالْفَتْحُ ۚ وَرَاَيْتَ النَّاسَ يَدْخُلُوْنَ فِىْ دِيْنِ اللهِ اَفْوَاجًا ۚ فَسَبِّحْ بِحَمْدِ رَبِّكَ وَاسْتَغْفِرْهُ ۚ اِنَّهٗ كَانَ تَوَّابًا ۚ

بِسْمِ اللهِ الرَّحْمٰنِ الرَّحِيْمِ

قُلْ يٰٓاَيُّهَا الْكٰفِرُوْنَ ۚ لَآ اَعْبُدُ مَا تَعْبُدُوْنَ ۚ وَلَآ اَنْتُمْ عٰبِدُوْنَ مَآ اَعْبُدُ ۚ وَلَآ اَنَا عَابِدٌ مَّا عَبَدْتُّمْ ۚ وَلَآ اَنْتُمْ عٰبِدُوْنَ مَآ اَعْبُدُ ۚ لَكُمْ دِيْنُكُمْ وَلِىَ دِيْنِ ۚ

بِسْمِ اللهِ الرَّحْمٰنِ الرَّحِيْمِ

اِنَّآ اَعْطَيْنٰكَ الْكَوْثَرَ ۚ فَصَلِّ لِرَبِّكَ وَانْحَرْ ۚ اِنَّ شَانِئَكَ هُوَ الْاَبْتَرُ ۚ

•▶ Read and memorise the Surahs.

Read one verse repeatedly to help memorise, then the next verse repeatedly. Join the two verses to test yourselves. Keep doing this until you learn the whole Surah.

- I can read the **Surahs from memory** fluently.
- I can implement all the lessons learnt previously into this exercise.

LESSON 45: LAST 10 SURAHS

بِسْمِ اللهِ الرَّحْمٰنِ الرَّحِيْمِ

اَرَءَيْتَ الَّذِىْ يُكَذِّبُ بِالدِّيْنِ ○ فَذٰلِكَ الَّذِىْ يَدُعُّ الْيَتِيْمَ ○ وَلَا يَحُضُّ عَلٰى طَعَامِ الْمِسْكِيْنِ ۗ فَوَيْلٌ لِّلْمُصَلِّيْنَ ○ الَّذِيْنَ هُمْ عَنْ صَلَاتِهِمْ سَاهُوْنَ ○ الَّذِيْنَ هُمْ يُرَآءُوْنَ ○ وَيَمْنَعُوْنَ الْمَاعُوْنَ ۗ

بِسْمِ اللهِ الرَّحْمٰنِ الرَّحِيْمِ

لِاِيْلَافِ قُرَيْشٍ ○ اٖلٰفِهِمْ رِحْلَةَ الشِّتَآءِ وَالصَّيْفِ ۗ فَلْيَعْبُدُوْا رَبَّ هٰذَا الْبَيْتِ ○ الَّذِىْٓ اَطْعَمَهُمْ مِّنْ جُوْعٍ ○ وَّاٰمَنَهُمْ مِّنْ خَوْفٍ ○

بِسْمِ اللهِ الرَّحْمٰنِ الرَّحِيْمِ

اَلَمْ تَرَ كَيْفَ فَعَلَ رَبُّكَ بِاَصْحٰبِ الْفِيْلِ ۗ اَلَمْ يَجْعَلْ كَيْدَهُمْ فِىْ تَضْلِيْلٍ ○ وَّاَرْسَلَ عَلَيْهِمْ طَيْرًا اَبَابِيْلَ ○ تَرْمِيْهِمْ بِحِجَارَةٍ مِّنْ سِجِّيْلٍ ○ فَجَعَلَهُمْ كَعَصْفٍ مَّاْكُوْلٍ ۗ

• Read and memorise the Surahs.

Read one verse repeatedly to help memorise, then the next verse repeatedly. Join the two verses to test yourselves. Keep doing this until you learn the whole Surah.

- I can read the Surahs from memory fluently.
- I can implement all the lessons learnt previously into this exercise.

Comments

STUDENT CHECKLIST

- I am able to read the entire Alphabet from memory.
- I am able to recognise all letters in different forms.
- I am able to read and spell words that have Fat-hah above them.
- I am able to read and spell words that have Kasrah beneath them.
- I am able to read and spell words that have Dhammah above them.
- I am able to read and spell words that have Fat-ha-tayn above them.
- I am able to read and spell words that have Kasra-tayn beneath them.
- I am able to read and spell words that have Dhamma-tayn above them.
- I am able to read and spell words that have Fat-hah followed by an Alif.
- I am able to read and spell words that have Madd Fat-hah above them.
- I am able to read and spell words that have Madd Kasrah beneath them.
- I am able to read and spell words that have Madd Dhammah above them.
- I am able to read and spell words that have Sukoon on them.
- I am able to read and spell words that have Fat-hah followed by a Waw Saakin.
- I am able to read and spell words that have Dhammah followed by a Waw Saakin.
- I am able to read and spell words that have Fat-hah followed by a Ya Saakin.
- I am able to read and spell words that have Kasrah followed by a Ya Saakin.

STUDENT CHECKLIST

- I am able to read and spell silent letters in words.
- I am able to read and spell the words that include a silent Alif.
- I am able to read and spell the special words used in the Qur'aan.
- I am able to read and spell words with a jerking sound.
- I am able to read and spell words that have Shaddah above them.
- I am able to read and spell words that have a small Madd.
- I am able to read and spell words that have a big Madd.
- I am able to read and spell words that have a big Madd followed a Shaddah.
- I am able to apply Qalqalah.
- I am able to apply Ghunnah.
- I am able to apply Izhaar.
- I am able to read the letter Ra as a Full Mouth/Empty Mouth Letter.
- I am able to read the word Allaah with a Full Mouth/Empty Mouth.
- I am able to apply Idghaam.
- I am able to apply Ikhfaa.
- I am able to apply the Meem Saakin rules.
- I am able to apply Iqlaab.
- I am able to read and spell words with Noon Qutni.
- I am able to apply all the Waqf Rules.
- I am able to apply Saktah and Waqfah.
- Advance stopping and joining
- Haroof Al Muqatta'aat / Waqf (Stopping)
- Complete Verse fluency
- Memorisation of the last 10 Surahs

Copyright of minimuallims publications.
All rights reserved. No part of this book may be reproduced in its current form without prior permission in writing from the minimuallims publications.

If you would like a copy of this book or would like to leave any feedback contact Shaykh Ubaid ur Rahman on info@minimuallims.com.